The Gift Of Prophecy

By Carlyle B. Haynes

Printed by
Remnant Publications, Inc.

The Gift of Prophecy

Cover Image Copyright© 1997
Photodisc, Inc.

This edition Published 1998

Copyright 1931
Southern Publishing Association

ISBN 1-883012-97-X

ARE YOU SEARCHING FOR TRUTH?

Do you need reliable answers to urgent questions?

- *Can we know and understand the future?*
- *What are the tests of a true prophet?*
- *Is the development of character important?*
- *Are there physical and spiritual laws for health and happiness?*
- *What really happens to us after death?*
- *Is it possible to live forever?*
- *How can you find inner peace in a world of chaos?*

Discover the answers to these and other vital questions by enrolling in our Bible Correspondence Course. We care about you and your welfare. Thats why we prepared this series of thought-provoking Bible study lessons to help people just like you. These lessons will stimulate you to think independently, and help you conscientiously make the choices which will make you happy.

The first two lessons in the series are free of charge. If you like the lessons, we ask you to include a nominal freewill offering, beginning with lesson three, to help cover postage and handling.

Do You Want To Know More?

Yes, Please send me, at no charge, the first two lessons.

Name_____

Address_____

City_____ State_____ Zip_____

Send to:

Bible Correspondence Course
P.O. Box 426
Coldwater, MI 49036   GOP 98

HOW IT ALL BEGAN

THE RISE AND FALL OF A CHOSEN NATION

THE HAPPINESS MILLIONS DESIRE IS FOUND IN THE MAN WHO DIVIDED HISTORY

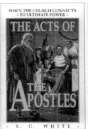
WHEN THE CHURCH CONNECTS TO ULTIMATE POWER

LOVE UNDER SEIGE

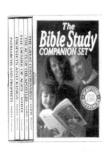

What makes this set so popular?
The Results!
Lifechanging Results

The Bible Study Companion Set   *$46.95

All five books together covering Genesis to Revelation — from the beginning of the universe through human history and on into our future. This set truly enriches your life.

Patriarchs and Prophets

Where did the human race come from? Why do bad things happen to good people? Why are babies born sick, and why do so many hard-working people never seem to get ahead? If God is good, why doesn't He prevent sadness and heartbreak? And if He is all-powerful, why doesn't He do something about evil and sickness? These questions and many more are answered in this remarkable book. Patriarchs and Prophets has brought peace and hope to millions throughout the world. *US$9.95

Prophets and Kings

Beginning with King Solomon, this book recounts the stories of great men and women of the Bible who lived from his reign to the first advent of Jesus Christ. Here you will read of Elijah, Daniel, Isaiah, and Jeremiah, among others–and you will find the lessons God would have us all learn from their lives. *US$9.95

The Desire of Ages

This book is about the Man who stands at the center of all human history. No one else has had such a profound influence on the people of this planet as Jesus Christ. *US$9.95

The Acts of the Apostles

This book is about power–ultimate power. The awesome power of the Holy Spirit, and what He can do in human lives when we surrender to be used by Him. When Pentecost came upon the early church, what God's people accomplished was miraculous. And all that the apostles did, God wants to do again through us today. *US$9.95

The Great Controversy

The world is on the verge of a stupendous crisis. Here is the authoritative answer to the confusion and despair of this tense age. Revealing God's ultimate plan for mankind, The Great Controversy may be the most important book you'll ever read. *US$9.95

These three books
will change your life...
...Forever

The Life–Giving Secrets Set   *$26.95

This three volume set will help you in your understanding the whole being–Physical, mental, and spiritual. With over 2,200 spiritual references, this set will make it simple to understand these Life–giving secrets.

Living the Life of the Lifegiver

Here is the most compelling book ever written on the parables of Jesus. Through familiar objects and incidents—the harvest, the shepherd, the builder, the traveler, the homemaker—Jesus linked divine truth with the common and ordinary. As you read this book, you will experience the sensation of walking through a door into a previously unseen but very real world. *US$9.95

Education

This book clearly reveals that love, the basis of creation and redemption, is the basis of true education. Simply put, changes that last are those that are motivated by unselfish love. *US$9.95

The Ministry of Healing

Using Jesus Christ as the example of the true Medical Missionary, this book, first written over 80 years ago, is an extraordinary example of medical-science prophecy. Many topics, such as mind cures, natural remedies, vegetarian diet, exercise, prenatal influences, and health education, are covered. The author speaks of true health and healing in conjunction with the powers of the Great Physician, Jesus Christ. *US$9.95

*All prices include postage and handling

Credit card orders, call: 800-423-1319

Send check or money order to:
Remnant Publications
P.O. Box 640, Coldwater, MI 49036

Contents

CHAPTER ONE

Communications of God to Men

FROM the beginning until now God has used many ways of communicating His will to man. So full and complete have been His revelations that mankind is indeed left without excuse.

When God first made man, He spoke to him face to face without restraint. Man was then pure and holy, and because of his sinlessness could endure thus to see and talk with Deity without being consumed.

In Eden man dwelt with God, and enjoyed with Him immediate, and not merely mediate, communication. If man had not fallen, he would have continued to enjoy this immediate intercourse. This open communication between God and man was broken off when man became a sinner.

Had man not fallen, paradise would have continued to lie about him through all coming centuries, as it lay about his infancy. Every man would have enjoyed direct vision of God and held immediate speech with Him. Man having fallen, the cherubim and the flame of a sword turning every way keep the path. And God has had to break His way in a roundabout fashion into the darkened hearts and minds of His creatures in order to reveal to them His redeeming grace and love.

It is sin that has made the breach between God and

man. Sin broke off this audible communication between the Creator and His creatures. It is because of sin that a Mediator was made necessary in the maintenance of any relation whatever between them.

"Your iniquities have separated between you and your God, and your sins have hid His face from you." Isa. 59:2.

No human being has ever seen the Father, or ever communicated with Him openly.

"The blessed and only Potentate, the King of kings, and Lords of lords; who only hath immortality, dwelling in the light which no man can approach unto; *whom no man hath seen, nor can see.*" 1 Tim. 6:15, 16.

This does not conflict with the statements in Ex. 24:9-11 that "Moses, and Aaron, Nadab, and Abihu, and seventy of the elders of Israel . . . saw the God of Israel," for "the God of Israel" whom they saw was the Jehovah of the Old Testament, who is the Christ of the New Testament.

It is Jesus who has made God known to man. It is Jesus who is the "one Mediator between God and men." (1 Timothy 2:5.)

It is Jesus, "who is the image of the invisible God," who shadowed the Father forth to the world. It is Jesus who is Creator, "for by Him were all things created, that are in heaven, and that are in earth, visible and invisible, whether they be thrones, or dominions, or principalities, or powers: all things were created by Him, and for Him." (Col. 1:16.)

It was this Mediator, Jesus Christ, who spoke the words of the ten-commandment law on Mount Sinai. The "law . . . was ordained by angels in the hand of a Mediator." Gal. 3:19. It was therefore the Lord Jesus who was seen on the mount by the leaders of Israel.

Through Christ, the channel of communication by

which Heaven speaks to earth, by which God reveals Himself to men, by which Divinity discloses its will to humanity, has been reopened. It was closed by sin. Jesus, the Redeemer, restores to man the privilege of communication with God.

He spoke as a Messenger of heaven.

"For I have not spoken of Myself; but the Father which sent Me, He gave Me a commandment, what I should say, and what I should speak." John 12:49.

Only three times, so far as the record goes, has the Father's voice been heard in this world. The first of these occasions was at the baptism of our Lord.

"Now when all the people were baptized, it came to pass, that Jesus also being baptized, and praying, the heaven was opened, and the Holy Ghost descended in a bodily shape like a dove upon Him, and a voice came from heaven, which said, Thou art My beloved Son; in Thee I am well pleased." Luke 3:21, 22.

The second occasion was at the transfiguration. There upon the mountain top, as the Lord stood with Peter, James, and John, "a bright cloud overshadowed them: and behold a voice out of the cloud, which said, This is My beloved Son, in whom I am well pleased; hear ye Him." (Matt. 17:5.)

The third occasion was during the crucifixion week, after the triumphal entry into Jerusalem, when the Greeks came to the temple and asked to see Jesus. At that time Jesus prayed, saying, "Father, glorify Thy Name. Then came there a voice from heaven, saying, I have both glorified it, and will glorify it again." John 12:28.

Aside from these three occasions, God the Father has not spoken audibly in this world.

But He has communicated His will to men. And in doing this He has used many agencies and means. "At

sundry times and in divers manners," He has communicated His revelations to men. (Hebrews 1:1.)

The Father has spoken through His Son, the Lord
Jesus. On many occasions His messages were brought to
earth by heavenly angels, and communicated by these
glorious beings directly to the persons for whom they
were sent.

Thus an angel brought a message from God to Hagar
(Gen. 16:7-12); to Lot (Gen. 19:1, 12, 13, 15); to
Abraham (Gen. 22:11, 12); to Moses (Ex. 3:2); to Balaam (Num. 22:32); to all the children of Israel
(Judges 2:1-4); to Gideon (Judges 6:11-18); to the
mother of Samson (Judges 13:3-5); to Elijah (1 Kings
19:5-7); to Daniel (Dan. 6:22); to Zechariah (Zech.
1:9, 11-14); to Joseph, husband of Mary (Matt. 1:20,
21; 2:13,19); to Zacharias, father of John the Baptist
(Luke 1:11-20); to Mary (Luke 1:26-38); to the shep-
herds (Luke 2:8-14); to the women at the tomb (Luke
24:23); to the apostles in jail (Acts 5:19, 20); to
Cornelius (Acts 10:3-6); to Peter in prison (Acts 12:7-
9); and to Paul (Acts 27:23, 24).

Another method that God used in ancient times to
communicate His will was by the Urim and Thummim. This is described in the Scripture in this way:

"And thou shalt put in the breastplate of judgment
the Urim and the Thummim; and they shall be upon
Aaron's heart, when he goeth in before the Lord." Ex.
28:30.

In some manner not clearly revealed in the Bible, God
revealed His will to the high priest by means of these
precious stones. We conclude from the meager evidence
that a light resting on the right stone meant a positive answer, and a cloud or shadow over the left one meant a
negative answer to the question asked by the high priest.

Another method that God used to make known His will was by the light between the cherubim on the mercy seat of the ark. This light the Jews called the Shekinah. Sometimes a voice from this light answered the high priest. A light here seemed to show approval and a shadow disapproval.

Still another method employed by God to disclose His will to men was that of dreams. He spoke to Abimelech "in a dream" (Gen. 20:3); to Laban (Gen. 31:24); to Joseph (Gen. 37:5); to Pharaoh (Gen. 41:7); to Solomon (1 Kings 3:5); and to Nebuchadnezzar (Dan. 2:1), as well as to many others.

These were all recognized as means by which God spoke to men. Indeed, when Saul, the king of Israel, "inquired of the Lord," and "the Lord answered him not, neither by dreams, nor by Urim, nor by prophets," Saul was convinced, as he states it himself, that "God is departed from me." (1 Sam. 28:6, 15.)

During the centuries, however, God has used one particular method more than any other by which to communicate His will to man. This has been prophecy. By the gift of prophecy, through the ages of the past, He has made known His commands and guided His people, and revealed His truth. Of this method of revealing His will He has said:

"Surely the Lord God will do nothing, but He revealeth His secret unto His servants the prophets." Amos 3:7.

It is this method in particular that will be discussed in the studies that follow in this book.

CHAPTER TWO

The Prophetic Gift

THE faculty of receiving a revelation from God and imparting it to men, either by speech or in writing, is a divine gift. It is spoken of in the Bible as "the gift of prophecy." It is one of the gifts of the Spirit conferred upon men for the upbuilding of God's work on earth.

"To one is given by the Spirit the word of wisdom; to another the word of knowledge by the same Spirit; to another faith by the same Spirit; to another the gifts of healing by the same Spirit; to another the working of miracles; to another prophecy; to another discerning of spirits; to another divers kinds of tongues; to another the interpretation of tongues." 1 Cor. 12:8-10.

These are all "given." They are "given by the Spirit." They are, therefore, gifts, "gifts of the Spirit." "Prophecy" is a gift, and is rightly known as "the gift of prophecy."

"Having then gifts differing according to the grace that is given to us, whether prophecy, let us prophesy according to the proportion of faith." Rom. 12:6.

It is plain that to speak of "the gift of prophecy" is to use an entirely Biblical expression. It is used in exactly that form, referring to one of the most valued gifts, in 1 Cor. 13:2.

The word translated "prophecy" in these passages has reference to predicting future events. In addition to that, however, it means to declare the will of heaven, to interpret the purposes of God, or to make known in any way the truth of God.

While one important meaning of prophecy is to predict or foretell future events, it must be remembered that those who were called to such work were primarily mouthpieces of God. With such predictions as they were given, they usually connected instructions and exhortations in regard to the sins, the danger, and the duties of men. Hence their office of "prophesying," and their gift of "prophecy," came to mean that which in any way communicated to man the will of God, in warning, in threatening, in instructing, in counseling, in admonishing, or in predicting, as well as in expressing devotional sentiments and praise.

These gifts of the Spirit are not given to all believers alike. They are distributed in accordance with the will of the Spirit.

"But all these worketh that one and the selfsame Spirit, dividing to every man severally as He will." 1 Cor. 12:11.

Conybeare's translation of this verse reads:

"But all these gifts are wrought by the working of that one and the same Spirit, who distributes them to each according to His will."

All the followers of Christ, therefore, do not have the same gift. Each one is endowed as the Spirit decides. He confers on each one that which He sees to be best and wise and helpful. He distributes those gifts as to Him seems best adapted to promote and foster and advance the welfare of the whole church.

Not all are apostles. Not all have the gift of prophecy. This is made plain by Paul.

"Are all apostles? Are all prophets? Are all teachers? Are all workers of miracles? Have all the gifts of healing? Do all speak with tongues? Do all interpret?" 1 Cor. 12:29, 30.

These questions imply, with pointed emphasis, that such a thing could not be, and ought not to be, and, in fact, did not exist, It was not true, as a clear matter of fact, that all were equal in relation to these gifts, or that all were qualified for offices which others were given, or that all possessed the same gift. Some were given the gift of apostleship; others were not. Some were given the gift of prophecy; others were not. Some were given the gift of teaching; others were not.

The gift of the Spirit, that is, the impartation of the greatest of all gifts, the Holy Spirit, is for all believers. "The manifestation of the Spirit is given to every man to profit withal." 1 Cor. 12:7. Here there is no difference. But in the impartation of the special gifts of the Spirit there is a most decided difference.

This question of the distribution of these special and important gifts is presented by Paul with most illuminating clearness. Conybeare gives his statements with exact fidelity to the Greek:

"Moreover, there are varieties of gifts, but the same Spirit gives them all; and [they are given for] various ministrations, but all to serve the same Lord; and the working whereby they are wrought is various, but all are wrought in all by the working of the same God. But the gift whereby the Spirit becomes manifest is given to each for the profit of all. To *one* is given by the Spirit the utterance of wisdom, to *another* the utterance of knowledge according to the working of the same Spirit. To *another* faith through the same Spirit. To *another* gifts of healing through the same Spirit. To *another* the powers which work miracles; to *another* prophecy; to *another* the discernment of Spirit; to *another* varieties of tongues; to *another* the interpretation of tongues." 1 Cor. 12:4-10.

Another Biblical expression for this special gift of the Spirit is "the spirit of prophecy." This is found in the following passage:

"And I fell at his feet to worship him. And he said unto me, See thou do it not: I am thy fellow servant, and of thy brethren that have the testimony of Jesus: worship God: for the testimony of Jesus is the spirit of prophecy." Rev. 19:10.

Later in this discussion we shall learn the identity of the speaker in this passage and catch the significance of this expression.

CHAPTER THREE

Spiritual Gifts in the Christian Church

READY and widespread acceptance among Christians has been given to the view that the gift of prophecy was exclusively an Old Testament manifestation, and does not belong to the Christian dispensation.

This is a mistake. The gift of prophecy is also decidedly a New Testament endowment. It was divinely given to the Church at its founding. It was expressly declared to be given for the entire duration of the Christian centuries. It is, as a *"gift of the Spirit,"* an integral part of the dispensation of the Spirit. It was designed to assist in bringing the Christian church to perfection. It was known and used in the days of the apostles. And its exercise, counsel, and leadership is one of the great needs of the Christian church at this time.

It was when Jesus, having completed the work for the salvation of men that He came to earth to accomplish, returned to heaven at His ascension that He gave to His church the gift of prophecy.

The foundation for His church had been laid in the saving work of His death, burial, resurrection, and ascension. After that, the building of His church was to be turned over to men, led by the Holy Spirit. And

these men were not qualified by any natural endowments, by any natural ability or wisdom, to successfully accomplish and bring to completion a spiritual
work. So He gave them spiritual endowments.

First, the greatest of all gifts was imparted. The
Spirit was given. He was to be the Head of the church
on earth. He was to be the Representative of God, the
Vicar of God, the Vicegerent of the Son of God among
men. Through the spiritual power He would impart to
men the church was to be built and completed.

And then He gave special gifts, to fit and prepare
men to do His work, to qualify them for success in
spiritual endeavors, to enable them to achieve His
purpose on the earth.

Paul discloses the time these gifts were made;
names some of the most important of the gifts; reveals
the purpose of their being given; and makes known
how long they were designed to remain in the church.

"When He ascended up on high, He led captivity
captive, and gave gifts to men. . . . And He gave some,
apostles; and some, prophets; and some, evangelists;
and some, pastors and teachers; for the perfecting of
the saints, for the work of the ministry, for the edifying of the body of Christ: till we all come in the unity
of the faith, and of the knowledge of the Son of God,
unto a perfect man, unto the measure of the stature of
the fullness of Christ; that we henceforth be no more
children, tossed to and fro, and carried about with every wind of doctrine, by the sleight of men, and cunning craftiness, whereby they lie in wait to deceive;
but speaking the truth in love, may grow up into Him
in all things, which is the Head, even Christ." Eph.
4:8-15.

This passage makes it plain that the gifts were

placed in the church at the time "when He ascended up on high."

The five gifts enumerated here as having been placed in the church at the beginning are those of apostles, prophets, evangelists, pastors, and teachers. It should be noted that the gift of prophecy did not expire with the Old Testament. It was needed in the Christian church at its founding. Being needed, it was given. It was given by the Head of the church Himself. It has a vital place in the work of the church.

The purpose for which gifts were given is fourfold, as covered in this passage. "For the perfecting of the saints," "for the work of the ministry," "for the edifying of the body of Christ," and "that we henceforth be no more children, tossed to and fro, and carried about with every wind of doctrine, by the sleight of men." That is, these gifts were designed for perfection, for service, for edification, and for unity. They were meant to develop the interior life of Christians; to inspire to, and impart ability for, Christian activity in service for others; to bring the church to completion in its development; and to bring about unity in faith and doctrine.

As none of these objectives is yet reached, every one of the gifts designed to reach them is still needed. Not one can be allowed to depart from the church without real loss to the church.

"For the perfecting of the saints"—perfection of life, of walk, of conduct, of experience, of service, of victory over sin. We are not there yet.

"For the work of the ministry," or, as Weymouth has it, "in order to fully equip His people for the work of serving." To make them as active in soul-winning endeavors as it is the purpose of God for them to be;

to make them skillful in speaking a word in season to the lost sinner; to equip them with spiritual power in their witness-bearing for Christ; to make their testimony powerful and efficacious; to inspire them to zeal and earnestness in Christian activity. Surely we still need all this done for us.

"For the edifying of the body of Christ." That is, for building up the church. For building it up in the knowledge of the truth, in piety, in order that everything in the church might be well-arranged, or put in its proper place, and that the church might be complete.

"That we henceforth be no more children, tossed to and fro, and carried about with every wind of doctrine." Weymouth puts it: "So we shall no longer be babes nor shall we resemble mariners tossed on the waves and carried about with every changing wind of doctrine according to men's cleverness and unscrupulous cunning, making use of every shifting doctrine to mislead, But we shall lovingly hold to the truth, and shall in all respects grow up into union with Him who is our Head, even Christ. Dependent on Him, the whole body—its various parts closely fitting and firmly adhering to one another—grows by the aid of every contributory link, with power proportioned to the need of each individual part, so as to build itself up in a spirit of love."

These gifts, then, are to enable Christians to put on the characteristics of manhood; to come to maturity; to arrive at that firmness in religious opinion which becomes maturity of life; to hold settled religious opinions; to carefully examine what is truth and, finding truth, to adhere to it; not to yield to every passing wind of doctrine, but lovingly hold to, and speak, the truth; meanwhile growing up into Him who is our Head, even Christ, depending on Him; learning of Him; following Him; abiding in Him; and thus being brought to perfection.

These gifts were meant to help in the accomplishment of these great and glorious purposes. They were placed in the church by our Lord himself. There is not one of them but is greatly needed, now as much as ever; now, perhaps, more than ever. We cannot let one of them go without grave loss.

The time during which these gifts were meant to remain in the church is clearly stated. "Till we all come in the unity of the faith, and of the knowledge of the Son of God, unto a perfect man, unto the measure of the stature of the fullness of Christ." That is, it was not in God's purpose that these gifts should be removed from the church before Christians had arrived at a state of complete unity and entire perfection. It is His design that His people shall all hold the same truth and have the same confidence in the Son of God. Even "unto a perfect man," the standard of that perfection being "the measure of the stature of the fullness of Christ."

The meaning here is not the teaching of sinless perfection, but of maturity. Paul is urging his readers out of the state of childhood into a state of grown-up, mature life. The gifts were conferred on the infant church that it might be brought to maturity, that it might become strong, stable, mature, vigorous, wise, and energetic. The stature it is to arrive at is that of Christ. He was to be its standard. The measure to be reached was Christ. It was to grow, and its individual members were to grow, until it and they were like Him. And the gifts of the Spirit were to remain in the church until this great objective becomes a reality.

It is not yet a reality. All these gifts, then, including the gift of prophecy, should still be in the true church of Christ.

CHAPTER FOUR

The Purpose of the Gifts

THE gifts of the Spirit were placed in the church when it was founded in order that its completion might be assured. Men could not carry on this sacred work alone. The church is a divine institution. It must have divine grace, divine wisdom, divine power, and divine leadership, if it accomplishes its divine purpose.

Human talents were not—are not—sufficient to assure success to the spiritual activities of the body of Christ. Human wisdom would surely result in disaster to the program of salvation. Something more was needed—and is still needed—in the church of Christ, than anything and all that men can contribute, if God's plans for His church are to be successfully consummated.

These considerations were, without doubt, in the thought of the divine Head of the church as the time drew near for His departure from the earth, and His return to heaven. He had given a great commission. His followers were to go into all the world, and take the gospel of His grace to every person. He had announced a great program, that of human salvation. He had made full provision in His own ministry, death, burial, and resurrection, for this salvation. He had declared that even the "gates of hell" would not prevail against His church, founded as it was upon Himself.

And now He, the Head, was about to depart. Most vital things to the salvation of men and the completion of the work of salvation required His presence in heaven. Was the church to be left alone, without divine leadership and divine help?

The leaders of the church were poor men, without scholarship, and without outstanding ability. They were of the peasant class, fishermen most of them. They had no prestige, no social standing or influence, certainly no political standing. The work they were engaged in already had brought, and would increasingly bring, upon them the opposition of the great and powerful social, religious, and political institutions of the world. They were not prepared, nor would any other group of men have been prepared, to take over the responsibility of leadership, unassisted by divine power, wisdom, and ability, in the church of the living God.

And so "for the perfecting of the saints, for the work of the ministry, for the edifying of the body of Christ" (Eph. 4:12), He "gave gifts to men," and "He himself appointed some to be apostles, some to be prophets, some to be evangelists, some to be pastors and teachers." Eph. 4:8, 11, Weymouth.

It was as though a great architect or contractor, having an imposing and important edifice to construct, drew his plans, employed workmen and superintendents, and then placed at their disposal all kinds of time - and labor-saving devices, delivered to them the specifications and plans, told them the length of time they had before the building must be completed, made every arrangement necessary, assembled all equipment necessary, provided all material necessary, and then placed the work in their hands for accomplishment, and took his departure for "a far country."

Suppose, instead of using the plans and equipment he had provided, the workmen had torn up the specifications, disregarded his provisions, scrapped his equipment and machinery, ignored his instructions, failed to use his materials, and gone about the task in their own way, without using anything he had provided?

This would be just about a parallel to the church's attempting to complete its building and finish the divine program on earth without the assistance of the gifts that God has given to do this very thing. These gifts were needed when they were first given, all of them; they are needed equally as much now, all of them. The church cannot finish its work in the world without their help and leadership.

When these gifts were all in the church, at the beginning of its witnessing, their influence unified the church as it has never been unified since. This is what the gifts were given to accomplish, that "we all attain unto the unity of the faith." Eph. 4:13, A.R.V. And the record is, when the gifts all manifested themselves, that "the multitude of them that believed were of one heart and of one soul." (Acts 4:32.) As a consequence of this unity there was great success in preaching the gospel, for "with great power gave the apostles witness of the resurrection of the Lord Jesus: and great grace was upon them all." (Acts 4:31-33.)

Surely as we read such a description of the early church we must realize how greatly to be desired such a condition is, and how different it is from the condition that prevails among Christians at the present time. Division, separation, false doctrines, perverted teachings, and widespread apostasy have come into the Christian church. There is little unity of belief, and little unity of effort. There never has been a time when there has been such great diversity of opinion and doctrine in Christendom as now.

Is it not clear that if the gifts of the Spirit were necessary to maintain the unity of the apostolic church, they are more necessary now to restore that unity to the scattered followers of the Lord Jesus? What is to bring about this unity in these days when the church is expecting its returning Lord but the gifts of the Spirit that were conferred upon the church for this very purpose?

"Apostles." The term apostle is not confined in the New Testament to the twelve, nor is the gift of apostleship limited to those first apostles. This word was in common use among the Jews, being given to the legate or officer who attended on various synagogues. It was especially bestowed on the messengers of the high priest or patriarch who went about collecting the temple tax paid by every Jew towards the support of the patriarch and the Sanhedrin. In its general use it meant a delegate, or envoy, or ambassador, accredited by some public authority, and charged with a special mission and message.

In the New Testament the word apostle is used in various ways. Sometimes it is limited to the twelve alone. At other times it has a wider and more general sense. In Acts 14:4, 14 it is used of Barnabas and Paul, who were not of the twelve. In 1 Thess. 2:6 it is used of Paul and his comrades. In Rom. 16:7 it is used of Andronicus and Junia. In 2 Cor. 8:23 the same

Greek word refers to Titus and others as "messengers of the churches." In 2 Cor. 11:13 "false apostles" are spoken of, meaning the emissaries of the circumcisionists among the Jews. False apostles are also referred to in Rev. 2:2. Our Lord himself is called an apostle in Heb. 3:1.

In John 13:16, "The servant is not greater than his lord; neither he that is sent greater than He that sent him," the words "he that is sent" are translated from the Greek word which elsewhere is translated "apostle." The same word in the Greek is translated "messengers" in 2 Cor. 8:23 and "messenger" in Philippians 2:25.

The gift of apostleship, then, is the gift of a pioneer, one who is sent as a messenger of Heaven and commissioned of God to open a new work, to break up the fallow ground, a frontiersman in extending the work of the kingdom. Every religious body has had its apostles, John and Charles Wesley for Methodism, Luther for Lutheranism, John Calvin and John Knox for Presbyterianism, Roger Williams for the Baptists. They still have them in their missionaries; for missionary work among primitive, heathen people surely requires this gift.

The various bodies constituting Protestant Christianity also believe in the gift of evangelists, pastors, and teachers. They avowedly claim to possess these four gifts, apostles, evangelists, pastors, and teachers.

But the passage under discussion names five gifts, not four. It speaks of apostles, *prophets,* evangelists, pastors, and teachers. These Protestant bodies neither claim nor possess the gift of prophecy.

Prophets are those who possess a divine gift of receiving from God *by revelation* His message for His people. Many Christian leaders teach that this gift has not been manifested in the church since apostolic times. But God declares it was placed in His church for all time, along with the other gifts that are acknowledged by all to still be in the church. The gift of prophecy belongs in the church now. To have its blessing and guidance and illumination would be of inestimable advantage to the church. What, then, has become of this gift? We shall arrive at the correct answer to this question as we continue this study.

> *"When He ascended up on high, He led captivity captive, and gave gifts unto men. And He gave some, apostles, and some, prophets; and some, evangelists; and some, pastors and teachers; for the perfecting of the saints, for the work of the ministry, for the edifying of the body of Christ: till we all come in the unity of the faith, and of the knowledge of the Son of God, unto a perfect man, unto the measure of the stature of the fullness of Christ."*
> *Eph. 4:9-13.*

CHAPTER FIVE

The Importance and Benefit of the Prophetic Gift

ALL of the gifts, of the Spirit, as we have seen, are of vital importance to the church and its work. "Apostles" is, of course, the gift of first importance, for it has to do with first things. Second only to that of "apostles" is the gift of prophecy, the gift that has been apparently lost in the church.

When the sacred writers discuss these gifts they do not always put them in the order of their importance. There is one place, however, where Paul does this, and this is it:

"And God hath set some in the church, *first* apostles, *secondarily* prophets, *thirdly* teachers, *after that* miracles, *then* gifts of healings, helps, governments, diversities of tongues." 1 Cor. 12:28.

It is good to have the mind of the Spirit on this matter of the relative importance, of the gifts. Left to our own judgment it is more than likely that we would have placed them in another order. The gift of prophecy is a gift of vital importance. We might not have known that, had the Spirit not made it plain. We might have thought that we were not losing much to be without the help of this gift. With this passage we know that the church would be losing, without this gift, something of inestimable value.

Nor is it likely that if we were left to arrange the gifts in the order of their importance, we would have put *"teachers"* third. "Miracles" and "gifts of healings" would, no doubt, have struck us as of superior importance. But, in the mind of the Spirit, the gift of teaching, that wonderful, God-given faculty of imparting to others the very mind and truth of God, is of paramount importance; more important, indeed, than healing the sick or performing a miracle. Yes, it is good to have the mind of the Spirit here.

The gift of prophecy is primarily for the benefit of the church.

"Wherefore tongues are for a sign, not to them that believe, but to them that believe not: but prophesying serveth not for them that believe not, but for them which believe." 1 Cor. 14:22.

Conybeare puts this more concisely in his translation:

"So that the gift of tongues is a sign given rather to unbelievers than to believers; whereas the gift of prophecy belongs to believers."

This is the reason why the church possessing the gift of prophecy does not say much about it among unbelievers. The instruction brought by this gift is peculiarly and specifically for the church. The light it imparts may be given to the world and bring great blessing, but primarily its testimony is for the church itself.

Consider some of the benefits this gift has conferred on the church. In nearly every great movement of reform in the church this gift has supplied the leadership. This was the case in the great deliverance from Egypt, and it has been the case repeatedly since.

"By a prophet the Lord brought Israel out of Egypt, and by a prophet was he preserved." Hosea 12:13.

Then, too, through the revelations made to those who have been permitted to exercise this gift, the future has been foretold.

"We have also a more sure word of prophecy; whereunto ye do well that ye take heed, as unto a light that shineth in a dark place, until the day dawn, and the day-star arise in your hearts." 2 Peter 1:19.

This certainly has been of great value and benefit to the church.

Above all, it has been through the operation of this gift that the Holy Bible has been given to the church, a benefit so great as to be beyond our power to estimate. A gifted Christian scholar and teacher has written this on the value of the Bible to the church and to the world:

"What, indeed, would the church be—what would we, as Christian men, be—without our inspired Bible? Many of us have, no doubt, read Jean Paul Richter's vision of a dead Christ, and have shuddered at his pictures of the woe of a world from which its Christ has been stolen away. It would be a theme worthy of some like genius to portray for us the vision of a dead Bible,—the vision of what this world of ours would be, had there been no living word of God cast into its troubled waters with its voice of power, crying 'Peace! Be still!' What does this Christian world of ours not owe to this Bible! And to this Bible conceived, not as a part of the world's literature,—the literary product of the earliest years of the church; not as a book in which, by searching, we may find God and perchance somewhat of God's will: but as the very word of God, instinct with divine life from the 'In the

beginning' of Genesis to the 'Amen' of the Apoca-
lypse,—breathed into by God, and breathing out God
to every devout reader. It is because men have so
thought of it that it has proved a leaven to leaven the
whole lump of the world. We do not half realize what
we owe to this book, thus trusted by men. We can
never fully realize it. For we cannot, even in thought,
unravel from this complex web of modern civilization
all the threads from the Bible which have been woven
into it, throughout the whole past, and now enter into
its very fabric. And, thank God, much less can we
ever untwine them in fact, and separate our modern
life from all those Bible influences by which alone it
is blessed, and sweetened, and made a life which men
may live.

"Dr. Gardiner Spring published, years ago, a series
of lectures in which he sought to take some account of
the world's obligations to the Bible,—tracing in turn
the services it has rendered to religion, to morals, to
social institutions, to civil and religious liberty, to the
freedom of slaves, to the emancipation of woman and
the sweetening of domestic life, to public and private
beneficence, to literary and scientific progress, and
the like. And Adolph Monod, in his own inimitable
style, has done something to awaken us as individuals
to what we owe to a fully trusted Bible, in the development of our character and religious life. In such
matters, however, we can trust our imaginations better
than our words, to remind us of the immensity of our
debt.

"Let it suffice to say that to a plenarily inspired
Bible, humbly trusted as such, we actually, and as a
matter of fact, owe all that has blessed our lives with
hopes of an immortality of bliss, and with the present

fruition of the love of God in Christ. This is not an exaggeration. We may say that without a Bible we might have had Christ and all that He stands for to our souls. Let us not say that this might not have been possible. But neither let us forget that, in point of fact, it is to the Bible that we owe it that we know Christ and are found in Him. And may it not be fairly doubted whether you and I,—however it may have been with others,—would have had Christ had there been no Bible? We must not at any rate forget those nineteen Christian centuries which stretch between us and Christ, whose Christian light we would do much to blot out and sink in a dreadful darkness if we could blot out the Bible. Even with the Bible, and all that had come from the Bible to form Christian lives and inform a Christian literature, after a millennium and a half the darkness had grown so deep that a Reformation was necessary if Christian truth was to persist,—a Luther was necessary, raised up by God to rediscover the Bible and give it back to man. Suppose there had been no Bible for Luther to rediscover, and on the lines of which to refound the church,—and no Bible in the hearts of God's saints and in the pages of Christian literature, persisting through those darker ages to prepare a Luther to rediscover it?

"Though Christ had come into the world and had lived and died for us, might it not be to us,—you and me, I mean, who are not learned historians but simple men and women,—might it not be to us as though He had not been? Or, if some faint echo of a Son of God offering salvation to men could still be faintly heard even by such dull ears as ours, sounding down the ages, who would have ears to catch the fullness of the message of free grace which He brought into the world? Who could assure our doubting souls that it was not all a pleasant dream? Who could cleanse the message from the ever-gathering corruptions of the multiplying years? No: whatever might possibly have been had there been no Bible, it is actually to the Bible that you and I owe it that we have a Christ,—a Christ to love, to trust, and to follow, a Christ without us the ground of our salvation, a Christ within us the hope of glory."—"*Revelation and Inspiration*," pp. 71-73, *by B. B. Warfield.*

And this blessed Book, with its comfort and hope, has come to us through the operation of the gift of prophecy.

"For the prophecy came not in old time by the will of man: but holy men of God spake as they were moved by the Holy Ghost,." 2 Pet. 1:21.

Surely, we cannot afford to let this precious gift of prophecy go, or get along without its divine instruction and leadership. We must learn how it has come about that this gift has been removed from the church, why it has not been manifested as constantly as some of the other gifts. If this is due to some failure or some transgression on the part of the church, for which God has removed this gift, let us learn what it is, and correct it. The church of Christ needs the benefit of this gift more today, perhaps, than ever before.

CHAPTER SIX

The Prophetic Gift Belongs to New Testament Christianity

THE manifestation of the gift of prophecy was not confined to the Old Testament. We have seen that it was among the gifts of the Spirit that were conferred upon the infant church. It is clear also that it was the purpose of God for this gift, with the others, to remain in the church to the very end. (Eph. 4:8-14.)

The manifestation of the gift of prophecy in New Testament times is a fulfillment of an Old Testament prophecy. Joel wrote:

"And it shall come to pass afterward, that I will pour out My Spirit upon all flesh; and your sons and your daughters shall prophesy, your old men shall dream dreams, your young men shall see visions." Joel 2:28.

It was this prophecy to which Peter directed attention as explaining the phenomena of Pentecost.

"These are not drunken," he said, "as ye suppose . . . but this is that which was spoken by the prophet Joel: And it shall come to pass in the last days, saith God, I will pour out My Spirit upon all flesh: and your sons and your daughters shall prophesy, and your young men shall see visions, and your old men shall dream dreams: and on My servants and on My handmaidens I will pour out in those days of My Spirit; and they shall prophesy." Acts 2:15-18.

Clearly the gift of prophecy did not expire with the days of the prophets of the Old Testament. At the very beginning of the work of Christ we are told of the prophecy of Simeon. (Luke 2:25-35.) "Anna, a *prophetess*," was also at that time in Jerusalem, and praised God for the privilege of seeing the infant Redeemer. (Luke 2:36-38.) Zacharias, the father of John the Baptist, is said to have "prophesied," and his prophecy is given. (Luke 1:67-79.)

That the gift of prophecy was known and operative in the days of the apostles is clear from a considerable number of passages. The record is that there "came prophets from Jerusalem unto Antioch. And there stood up one of them named Agabus, and signified by the Spirit that there should be great dearth throughout all the world; which came to pass in the days of Claudius Caesar." Acts 11:27, 28.

Some of the prophets of the New Testament are named by the writer of the Acts.

"Now there were in the church that was at Antioch certain prophets and teachers; as Barnabas, and Simeon that was called Niger, and Lucius of Cyrene, and Manaen." Acts 13:1.

"And Judas and Silas, being prophets also themselves, exhorted the brethren with many words, and confirmed them." Acts 15:32.

In Ephesus, when Paul baptized and laid his hands on certain disciples of the Lord, "they spake with tongues and prophesied." (Acts 19:6.)

As in the Old Testament, so in the New, the gift was not given exclusively to men, but to women as well. Speaking of Philip, the evangelist, Luke writes:

"The same man had four daughters, virgins, which did prophesy." Acts 21:9.

An incident in Paul's ministry in which the gift manifested itself, is thus described:

"There came down from Judea a certain prophet, named Agabus. And when he was come unto us, he took Paul's girdle, and bound his own hands and feet, and said, Thus saith the Holy Ghost, so shall the Jews at Jerusalem bind the man that owneth this girdle, and shall deliver him into the hands of the Gentiles." Acts 21:10, 11. And we know it was a true prophecy.

Instruction for regulating the exercise of the gift of prophecy in the church by both men and women is given by Paul in 1 Cor. 11:4, 5.

Believers are encouraged in 1 Cor. 14:1-5, to desire and highly value the gift of prophecy, and instruction regarding its exercise is given in much detail in the remaining verses of this chapter.

Paul, in writing to the Ephesians, makes it plain that prophets were associated with the apostles of Christ.

"Which in other ages was not made known unto the sons of men, as it is now revealed unto his holy apostles and *prophets* by the Spirit." Eph. 3:5.

And the attitude that believers are to take towards this gift is thus stated:

"Despise not prophesyings. Prove all things; hold fast that which is good." 1 Thess. 5:20, 21.

Some earnest believers, however, find certain passages of Scripture sources of perplexity in this connection. They are persuaded from the superficial perusal of them to believe that the gifts of the Spirit, especially that of prophecy, passed away with the apostles, and ceased with that generation. It will be helpful here to discuss these passages briefly, meanwhile asking God to shed light upon their true meaning.

One passage which has caused some to doubt the perpetuity of the gift of prophecy is this:

"Charity never faileth: but whether there be prophecies, they shall fail; whether there be tongues, they shall cease; whether there be knowledge, it shall vanish away. For we know in part, and we prophesy in part." 1 Cor. 13:8, 9.

Indeed, this passage does foretell the cessation of the gifts. It foretells also the vanishing away of knowledge. But the reader should not stop there in his reading but read on to learn *when* the gifts are to cease. The passage reveals this.

"But *when that which is perfect is come, then* that which is in part shall be done away. When I was a child, I spake as a child, I understood as a child, I thought as a child: but when I became a man, I put away childish things. For *now* we see through a glass, darkly; but *then* face to face: *now* I know in part; but *then* shall know even as also I am known." 1 Cor. 13:10, 11.

Hence it is clear that the gifts of the Spirit are to cease, and vanish away, only when "that which is perfect is come"; when we see "face to face"; when we "know even as also we are known." That will be at the perfect day of the return of our Lord.

This verse, then, instead of being ambiguous, adds clear testimony to other passages, and shows that the gifts that God set in the church at the beginning to bring us all into the unity of the faith, will not be taken away from the church until their purpose is accomplished, until the faith and hope of the church are realized, until the surpassing glory of the immortal state shall far outshine the most brilliant displays of spiritual power and knowledge by the gifts of the Spirit in this mortal state.

The abolition of spiritual gifts, especially the gift of prophecy, is also thought by some to be implied in the following language:

"I testify unto every man that heareth the words of the prophecy of this book, If any man shall add unto these things, God shall add unto him the plagues that are written in this book: and if any man shall take away from the words of the book of this prophecy, God shall take away his part out of the book of life."

This passage cannot mean that all prophesying after John's time must be false, and that God hereby states that He will never communicate anything after John's time through the gift of prophecy. John himself wrote his gospel after these visions on the isle of Patmos. He did not thereby add to the words of the prophecy of the Book of Revelation.

This caution against adding to or taking from, does not refer to the Bible as a complete book, but to the Book of Revelation as a separate book. It was not to be changed as it came from the hand of the apostle. Equally true it is, of course, that no man has a right to add anything to, or take anything from, any of the other books of the Bible. But John, when he wrote the Revelation, was not adding to, or taking from, the book of Daniel, for instance.

Revelation corroborates Daniel, giving much additional light upon the subject matter of that book. The passage under discussion sounds a warning against altering the word of God. It does not mean that God has bound Himself to keep silence; He is still at liberty to speak, and to employ the gift of prophecy in speaking.

All the gifts, therefore, are still available to the church of God. They have not passed away or ceased. The church should still give heed to Paul's earnest admonition:

"Follow earnestly after Love: yet delight in the spiritual gifts, but especially in the gift of Prophecy." 1 Cor. 14:1, Conybeare.

CHAPTER SEVEN

The Voice of God to His Church

THE gift of prophecy is the infallible and authoritative voice of God in this world. It is through this medium He has chosen to speak, and what He speaks in this way is from God, not man, and therefore infallible.

Infallibility does not belong to the prophet, or the prophetess, who brings the message. It belongs to the message brought. We do not believe in infallible men or women. We do believe in an infallible God who can make His will known to men with certainty and exactness.

The Hebrew name for "prophet" *(Nabhi)* means simply "spokesman," God's spokesman. It was characteristic of the prophets to announce their message by saying: "The word of Jehovah came to me," or just simply, "Saith Jehovah." Never does a prophet put his message forward as his own message. That he possesses the gift of prophecy at all is due not to any choice of his own, but wholly to a call of God, which in some cases was obeyed reluctantly. He prophesies or refrains from prophesying not at all in accordance with his own desires or choice but altogether as Jehovah opens and shuts his mouth and formulates his message for him, creating "the fruit of the lips."

"I will make thy tongue cleave to the roof of thy mouth, that thou shalt be dumb . . . but when I speak with thee, I will open thy mouth, and thou shalt say unto them, Thus saith the Lord God; He that heareth, let him hear; and he that forbeareth, let him forbear; for they are a rebellious house." Ezek. 3:26, 27.

"I create the fruit of the lips." Isa. 57:19.

"The Lord God hath given me the tongue of the learned, that I should know how to speak a word in season to him that is weary: He wakeneth morning by morning, He wakeneth mine ear to hear as the learned. The Lord God hath opened mine ear, and I was not rebellious." Isa. 50:4, 5.

The prophet of the Lord, in contrast with false prophets, vigorously claims that he does not speak out of his own heart (Ezek. 13:17), but that all he proclaims is the pure word of the Lord.

This is, indeed, the fundamental claim of the prophets, that the revelations made through them are not their own but wholly from God. Peter emphasizes this when he declares:

"No prophecy of Scripture is of private interpretation. For no prophecy ever was brought by the will of man; but men spake from God, being moved by the Holy Spirit." 2 Pet. 1:20, 21, R. V., margin.

Weymouth puts it: "Never did any prophecy come by human will, but men sent by God spoke as they were impelled by the Holy Spirit."

Goodspeed has it, "No prophecy ever originated in the human will, but under the influence of the Holy Spirit man spoke from God."

And Moffatt translates it, "Prophecy never came by human impulse, it was when carried away by the Holy Spirit that the holy men of God spoke."

It must not be understood that the human powers of the person have no part in receiving and imparting the divine message. That is not what I desire to imply. The intelligence of the prophet is not inactive. It is by means of their intelligence that they receive the message, and it thus becomes the instrument of revelation. What I do desire to emphasize is that their intelligence has no part in producing the message. Their intelligence *receives* it; it does not *produce* it. The message is *given to* the prophet; the prophet has no part in *creating* the message. The natural powers of the prophet are active in *receiving* the message; but passive so far as *creating* it is concerned. They are in no sense co-authors with God of their messages. The messages are given them, given them entire. That is, God speaks through them. They are more than His messengers: they are "His mouth."

At the same time their intelligence is active in the reception, the retention, the announcing of these messages. It contributes nothing to them, but constitutes a fit instrument for communicating them.

Why should it be thought incredible for God to be able to frame His own message in the language of the organs of His servants without that message thereby ceasing to be purely His message because it is expressed in a fashion natural to these organs? Certainly it seems to lie in the very nature of the case that if God makes a revelation to men He would make it in the language of men. More, He would do it in the language of the person He employs as the agent of His revelation, and that could mean not merely the language of this person's nation, or of his particular circle, but his own particular and, perhaps, peculiar language, inclusive of all that gives individuality to his self-expression. These peculiarities of expression would in no way affect the purity of the message as a direct communication from God.

Every message coming through the gift of prophecy, then, should be viewed as deriving its intellectual and spiritual quality, and its importance as a revelation, not from the messenger but from its Divine Author.

The prophet is but an agent to bring a message. The importance is in the message, not the messenger. The message is God's voice to men. The messenger is simply the agent selected of God through whom to send His message. The messenger is entirely human, and liable, when not under divine control, to err. The message is divine, and safeguarded from error by God.

To believe in the "infallibility of the pope" one must believe in the inerrancy of a person because of the power and authority with which that person is said to be clothed. To believe in the infallibility of the gift of prophecy is not to believe any person is inerrant, but only to recognize that God has established a gift by which He can make His will known to men without error. Authority and inerrancy are not in the person; they are in the gift, which is entirely controlled by God.

The person who has the gift is like any other person blessed with a divine gift. An evangelist has a divine gift, a pastor, a teacher. They are not, because of these gifts, separated from humanity. They are agents through whom God works. They are still human, still liable to err in all ordinary human relations and contacts. They are clothed with no super-human authority. They are worthy of no super-human honors. But the gift they exercise is to be heeded and honored, for that is divine.

CHAPTER EIGHT

God's Way of Communicating Truth

THE doctrine of "the infallibility of the pope" is a substitute for, and a counterfeit of, the truth regarding the gift of prophecy. Catholicism as a whole is a gigantic counterfeit of Christianity. Every truth in the gospel has its counterfeit in this false system. Along with the others the gift of prophecy is counterfeited.

The official doctrine regarding the pope's infallibility is that "by virtue of his supreme apostolic authority," when the occupant of Peter's chair "speaks *ex cathedra*" and "defines a doctrine regarding faith or morals," then "by the divine assistance promised to him in blessed Peter" his pronouncements are infallible.

It is apparent that this claim of infallibility is based upon the assumed position of the pope as successor of Peter. This is known as the doctrine of "apostolic succession." Because he sits in Peter's chair, and the succession as head of the church is alleged to have come down to him from Peter without break, therefore he is clothed with infallibility.

This is a false "succession." It cannot be traced back to Peter. And if it could, Peter had no such headship, or authority, as is claimed for the pope.

But there is a true succession by which truth comes infallibly from God to man, of which this false succession is but a counterfeit. This true succession is thus revealed in the Scriptures:

"The Revelation of Jesus Christ, which God gave unto Him, to show unto His servants things which must shortly come to pass; and He sent and signified it by His angel unto His servant John." Rev. 1:1.

John, in turn, was bidden to write to the "angels" of the seven churches.

Here is the true succession by which truth, originating with God, is transmitted, without error, from God to man: God, Christ, "His angel," those who have the gift of prophecy (called here "His servants"), the ministry, the churches.

When truth is transmitted in this way, it comes to men infallibly correct; for this is God's way.

According to this passage the message to be sent to men originated with God. He gives it to Christ. Christ gives it to "His angel." The angel transmits it to those who possess the gift of prophecy. They, in turn, pass it on to the churches through the ministry. That is God's method of transmitting His truth.

It will be of interest here to inquire into the identity of the being spoken of in the passage as "His angel." This is without question a particular angel, one who has been given charge of the important work of transmitting the messages of Heaven that are communicated to earth through the medium of the gift of prophecy.

This angel is the last link on the heavenly side in this important matter of the communication of truth to men; and the gift of prophecy is the connecting link on the earthly side. "His angel" communicates directly to the prophet or prophetess.

It seems clear from many Scriptures passages that one particular angel has charge of this work, and is therefore spoken of as "His angel." The visions of Daniel were given him by the angel Gabriel.

"And I heard a man's voice . . . which called, and said, Gabriel, make this man to understand the vision." Dan. 8:16.

It was this same angel, Gabriel, who, more than five hundred years later, announced the imminent advent of our Lord and His forerunner, John.

"And there appeared unto him [Zacharias] an angel of the Lord. . . . The angel said unto him, Fear not, Zacharias: for thy prayer is heard; and thy wife Elisabeth shall bear thee a son, and thou shalt call his name John. . . . And the angel answering said unto him, I am Gabriel, that stand in the presence of God; and am sent to speak unto thee, and to show thee these glad tidings." Luke 1:11, 13, 19).

Later the same angel visited Mary, the mother of our Lord.

"And in the sixth month the angel Gabriel was sent from God unto a city of Galilee, named Nazareth, to a virgin espoused to a man whose name was Joseph, of the house of David; and the virgin's name was Mary. . . . And the angel said unto her, Fear not, Mary: . . . thou shalt conceive in thy womb, and bring forth a son, and shalt call His name JESUS." Luke 1:26, 27, 30.

It is, without doubt, this same angel Gabriel who imparted to John on the isle of Patmos the instruction contained in the book of Revelation, mentioned as "His angel" in Revelation 1:1, and who thus speaks of his own position and work:

"I fell at his feet to worship him. And he said unto

me, See thou do it not; I am thy fellowservant, and of
thy brethren that have the testimony of Jesus: worship
God: for the testimony of Jesus is the spirit of prophecy." Rev. 19:10.

Of this same angel who has charge of the gift of
prophecy Jesus himself says:

"I Jesus have sent *mine angel* to testify unto you
these things in the churches." Rev. 22:16.

This passage answers the question, "What is testimony?" The testimonies for the church constitute the
messages brought by the angel Gabriel from God and
from Christ for the people of God. Testimonies originate further back than the prophet. It is not the testimony of the prophet. It is the testimony of God. "I
Jesus have sent mine angel to *testify*." That which the
angel testifies is testimony. The prophet merely receives it and passes it on; he does not originate it.

"To testify these things *in the* churches." The testimony of the angel, then, imparting the messages of
heaven, becomes "Testimonies for the Church."

Clearly it is Gabriel who is God's messenger
between heaven and earth, bearing the messages of the
gift of prophecy.

"Whiles I was speaking in prayer, even the man
Gabriel, whom I had seen in the vision at the beginning, *being caused to fly swiftly,* touched me about the
time of the evening oblation. And he informed me,
and talked with me, and said, O Daniel, I am now
come forth to give thee skill and understanding." Dan.
9:21, 22.

This glorious and mighty being explains his own
relationship to his Lord, and his position in His
counsels in this way:

"But I will show thee that which is noted in the

Scripture of truth: and there is none that holdeth with me in these things, but Michael your prince." Dan. 10:21.

Michael is Christ. Gabriel is Christ's angel. And he has "the testimony of Jesus," which is "the spirit of prophecy."

CHAPTER NINE

Why the Prophetic Gift Was Removed

IT has been made clear in this series of studies that the gift of prophecy was placed in the Christian church at its beginning, being one of the gifts of the Spirit.

It was known and operative among the early Christians. It is clearly stated to have been in God's purpose for it, with the other gifts, to continue in the church "till we all come in the unity of the faith," that is, until the end of the witnessing of the church on earth.

This purpose has in some way been thwarted. For some reason the gift was removed and did not manifest itself for centuries so far as we have any record. Among the prominent denominations of Protestant Christianity it is unknown. While they recognize and claim the other gifts,—those of apostles, evangelists, pastors, and teachers,—they ignore the gift of prophecy, and lay no claim to its possession. For so many centuries has its voice been silent, its blessing withheld, and its leadership unknown, that they do not even realize they have suffered any loss.

But they have suffered a loss beyond our power to estimate. The churches are divided as never before in history, divided in spirit, in life, in doctrine, in polity, in action, and in program. They neither know what is coming upon the world, nor whither they themselves are drifting. They have no positive message for the world. They are without vision, without spiritual eye-sight. Anciently the prophet was called a "seer." (1 Sam. 9:9.) The seers were the eyes of the church. To-day the churches are without the gift of prophecy. They are without a "seer," without eyes, blind leaders of the blind. They neither know nor see where they are going.

All Christians would do well to search the Scriptures and learn why it is that the gift of prophecy has been removed, and the conditions of its restoration. For surely the Bible must throw some light upon this situation.

A connection full of significance between the possession of the gift of prophecy and obedience to the law of God is evident in many passages of the Bible. These two things, "the law and the prophets," are joined together throughout the Scriptures.

Predicting the overthrow, desolation, and captivity of Israel, Ezekiel wrote:

"Mischief shall come upon mischief, and rumor shall be upon rumor; then shall they seek a vision of the prophet; but the law shall perish from the priest, and counsel from the ancients." Ezek. 7:26.

Here the explanation is made that the reason why instruction through the gift of prophecy is not given is because the law is perished; that is, has not been observed, has been ignored. The implication is plain that the disobedience of the people to the law, especially when that disobedience has become general, widespread, and pronounced, will result in the withdrawal of the gift of prophecy.

"Where there is no vision, the people perish: but he that keepeth the law, happy is he." Prov. 29:18.

The teaching here seems plain that those who keep the law may confidently expect to have the benefit of visions, or instruction received through the gift of prophecy.

Lamenting the destruction of his beautiful and beloved city, Jerusalem, Jeremiah wrote:

"Her gates are sunk into the ground; he hath destroyed and broken her bars: her king and her princes are among the Gentiles: the law is no more; her prophets also find no vision from the Lord." Lam. 2:9.

Here, again, the "law" and the "prophets" are united. The reason "her prophets find no vision from the Lord" is obviously because "the law is no more"; that is, because they were not keeping it. Not only was the gift of prophecy removed on this account, but the record is, regarding the kingdom of Israel:

"Now for a long season Israel hath been without the true God, and without a teaching priest, and without law." 2 Chron. 15:3.

In the New Testament as well the same two things are constantly referred to together, "the law and the prophets."

"Think not that I am come to destroy the law, or the prophets." Matt. 5:17.

"For this is the law and the prophets." Matt. 7:12.

"On these two commandments hang all the law and the prophets." Matt. 22:40.

"We have found Him, of whom Moses in the law, and the prophets, did write." John 1:45.

"After the reading of the law and the prophets."

Acts 13:15.

"Believing all things which are written in the law and in the prophets." Acts 24:14.

"Persuading them concerning Jesus, both out of the law of Moses, and out of the prophets." Acts 28:23.

"Being witnessed by the law and the prophets." Rom. 3:21.

Ezekiel writes of a time in the history of Israel when "certain of the elders of Israel came to inquire of the Lord, and sat before me." (Ezek. 20:1.)

They came to Ezekiel when they wanted to inquire of the Lord, because they knew him to be God's spokesman, possessing the gift of prophecy.

And through Ezekiel God spoke to these leaders of Israel:

"Thus saith the Lord God; Are ye come to inquire of Me? As I live, saith the Lord God, I will not be inquired of by you." Ezek. 20:3.

The reasons why God would not give them the benefit of a response to their inquiry through the gift of prophecy are then set forth in detail. Among these reasons the following words are found:

"Because they despised My judgments, and walked not in My statutes, but *polluted My Sabbaths:* for their heart went after their idols." Verse 16.

"I gave them My sabbaths to be a sign between Me and them, that they might know that I am the Lord that sanctify them. But the house of Israel rebelled against Me: . . . they walked not in My statutes, and they despised My judgments, . . . and *My sabbaths they greatly polluted.*" Verses 12, 13.

"I am the Lord your God; walk in My statutes, and keep My judgments, and do them; *and hallow My sabbaths;* and they shall be a sign between Me and you, that ye may know that I am the Lord your God. Notwithstanding the children rebelled against Me: they walked not in My statutes, neither kept My judgments, . . . *they polluted My sabbaths.*" Verses 18-21.

In submitting the reasons why He was withdrawing the gift of prophecy from His people the Lord especially emphasizes the Sabbath. They were violating His law with special reference to Sabbath keeping. They had become a nation of Sabbath breakers. This was an evidence of apostasy from Him and His truth. It was a departure from the faith. It was an abandonment of His leadership. They thereby removed themselves from Him; and He removed from them the gift of prophecy.

These passages throw light upon the reasons for the removal of this important gift from the Christian church. We shall see what that light reveals.

CHAPTER TEN

The Prophetic Gift to Be Restored

SHORTLY after the days of the apostles the church departed from the law of God. As a consequence the gift of prophecy was removed.

Scarcely had the apostles been removed by death than the truths of the gospel began to be perverted. The essential teachings of the church, the very doctrines of the atonement, began, little by little, to change their form. This continued until they were wholly perverted. Paul had plainly warned the elders that "of your own selves [that is, from among the leaders of the church] shall men arise, speaking perverse things." Acts 20:30. That is, they would take the very truths of the gospel, and twist, change, warp, and pervert them, until they made them mean what they were never designed to mean. They would "change the truth of God into a lie." They would take every truth of the gospel and so interpret these truths as to make them teach falsehood. They would then substitute that falsehood for the truth of God.

Memorial days of saints, the worship of the Virgin Mary, and nearly every other error of Roman Catholicism, were introduced, at least in rudimentary form, during the days following the death of the apostles. Among these errors and perversions was the change that was made in the observance of the Sabbath from the seventh day of the week to the first. This change had its origin in the apostasy that was taking place in the church at that time.

Christ had observed the seventh day as the Sabbath. The apostles had observed the seventh day. The early Christians in the churches established by the apostles had observed the seventh day. Now a change was being made. The law of God was being set aside. As in former times among the Jews, the whole church was turning away from the Sabbath of the Lord.

General apostasy, widespread corruption, followed. The church departed from its true Head, forsook the teachings of the Holy Scriptures, and adopted strange notions, fanciful superstitions, pagan customs, false observances, and a counterfeit Sabbath.

The church departed so far from Christ that it became the exact opposite of that which it had been when first established. In the prophecy of the seven seals the color *white is* used to describe the church at its beginning. During the period of apostasy, which we are now considering, it was necessary for God to use *black* to describe the apostate condition. The church's beautiful robe of spotless white, the righteousness of Christ, had been laid aside, and it was endeavoring to gain a righteousness of its own, which in God's sight was hideous, and an insult to His Son.

All the truths with which God had endowed the church had been perverted and changed into falsehoods. The very benefits that He had conferred upon the church, and that He designed the church should in turn give freely to the world for the salvation of men, were prostituted to the gain of a fallen priesthood, and sold for money. The divine Head of the church was

driven out and a human head established. The divine
priesthood of our Lord was ignored and a human
priesthood inaugurated. The divine guidance of the
Spirit was refused and a human system was substituted.

Of course God removed the gifts of the Spirit from
the corrupt and apostate church, and among them the
gift of prophecy.

Protestantism, in the great Reformation of the six-
teenth century, rejected most of these perversions and
corruptions of the apostasy.

Protestantism was a return to, and a restoration of,
primitive Christianity. Catholicism had brought in
foreign and heathen elements and thus corrupted and
perverted the faith of the church, so that the religion
established by Christ had been obscured and lost. This
mixture of corrupt Christian doctrines with pagan
teachings and practices had been substituted for
genuine Christianity. Protestantism threw aside the
encrustations of centuries, rediscovered the original
truth of the gospel, abandoned the falsehoods and
frauds of the fallen church, and set forth "the Bible
and the Bible alone" as the sole source of truth for the
church.

And God restored the gifts of the Spirit. But not all
of them. There was one which is peculiarly and
closely connected with obedience to God's law. And
that law was not yet obeyed by Protestantism.

Great and glorious as the Reformation was, the
divine purpose for it has not yet been carried out. That
purpose was a full restoration and recovery of all the
truths of the gospel that had been perverted and lost
under the errors of Rome, among them the observance
of the Sabbath. This purpose has been delayed by the

formation of creeds and the establishment of denominations upon only such parts of the recovered gospel as were revealed to individual reformers.

If the great principles upon which the Reformation had been started had been steadily maintained, all truth would by now have been restored, and the churches of Christ would not now be in the deplorable condition they are. Instead of this, however, multitudes have been content to array themselves under the banner of some inadequate creed, which, though it may contain some truth, contains but a small part of that which the Lord has to reveal to His people. From the beginning of the Reformation God has had more truth and light to reveal to men than men placed in the creeds that they formed out of the teachings of Luther, Knox, Calvin, or Wesley. God did not reveal all He had to disclose to the world to these men or their followers, for He allows light to shine only as His servants can bear it. And for men to gather into a creed the teachings of the great Reformers, and take the position that they can accept and believe only what such creeds contain, is for them to shut themselves out from all the additional light and truth that God yet has to reveal to the world, and that is not contained in these creeds.

And as the Protestant churches did not restore the ancient Sabbath to its rightful place in their practice, so God did not restore to them the gift of prophecy.

From these considerations it is plain that when a body of people should arise that would take hold of all the truth of God, the Sabbath among all the other truths, it is reasonable to expect the Lord would restore to them the gift of prophecy. Indeed, this is exactly what is predicted in the word of God.

On the isle of Patmos John was shown the entire history of the church of Christ in advance. He saw its trials and its final victory. The church was displayed before him as a "woman clothed with the sun." (Revelation 12:1.) He saw the attempt of earthly rulers to destroy the Lord (Verses 3-5); the flight of the church into the wilderness to escape the persecution of Rome (verses 13, 14); the 1260 years of this persecution (verse 14); the help which the kingdoms of the earth gave to the church during the Reformation (verse 16); and then he was shown the last end of the church, the remnant church, the church just before the coming of the Lord. This true church of the Lord just before the Lord's second coming is identified by two characteristics:

"And the dragon was wroth with the woman, and went to make war with the remnant of her seed, *which keep the commandments of God, and have the testimony of Jesus Christ.*" Rev. 12:17.

The last church on earth, then, is to be a commandment-keeping church. This must include in its meaning that it will be a Sabbath-keeping church. No church which keeps but nine of the ten commandments can ever rightly be called a commandment-keeping church. It must observe all ten of the commandments to be thus designated.

This prophecy surely teaches that in the last days God will have a church that will believe and practice a complete gospel. In its practice the observance of the true, seventh-day Sabbath will be restored.

And to that church God will restore the gift of prophecy.

This is clearly the meaning of the other characteristic identifying the true church given in this passage.

It will not only "keep the commandments of God"; it will also "have the testimony of Jesus Christ." Rev. 19:10 declares the "testimony of Jesus" to be "the spirit of Prophecy."

Two things, then, will mark as genuine the church of Christ before the coming of our Lord. It will be a commandment-keeping church, a Sabbath-keeping church; and it will have restored to it the gift of prophecy. This is definitely and positively predicted in the word of God.

This view is confirmed by the language of Paul to the Corinthians. He wrote:

"I thank my God always on your behalf, for the grace of God which is given you by Jesus Christ; that in everything ye are enriched by Him, in all utterance, and in all knowledge; even as the testimony of Christ was confirmed in you; so that *ye come behind in no gift waiting for the coming of our Lord Jesus Christ.*" 1 Cor. 1:4-7.

From this it is clear that one of the characteristics of the church that is waiting for the coming of the Lord Jesus is that it *"come behind in no gift."*

The fulfillment of this important prediction of Rev. 12:17 in our day we shall cover as these studies are continued.

CHAPTER ELEVEN

Visions and Dreams

THE method by which God conveys to the mind and intellect of his servants, the prophets, the instruction that He desires imparted to His people is clearly described in the Bible. It is a method that God not only chooses to use for this purpose, but that, in using, He fully controls, so that there is no diversion of attention on the part of the recipient of the revelation, and therefore no corruption of the content of the revelation.

"Hear now My words: If there be a prophet among you, I the Lord will make Myself known unto him in a vision, and will speak unto him in a dream." Num. 12:6.

To us, visions and dreams may appear illfitted to serve as vehicles for divine communications. We may not be able to discern God's reasons for choosing them. But that He has chosen them is certain. This passage, together with many others, makes that clear. And some of the excellences of this method we can, with a little consideration, perceive.

It would seem clear that revelations rise in rank in proportion to the degree of completeness of the engagement of the attention, or mental activity, of the recipient in their reception. In a vision or divinely given dream, images or ideas, either filling the mind or passing in procession before the consciousness, completely engage the attention of the person without admixture of other thoughts. The mind is thus entirely in the control of the agency making the revelation. And it should be pointed out in this connection that such revelations, together with their contents, are determined by a power outside the recipient's own will. The intellectual or spiritual quality of a revelation thus received is not derived from the recipient but from its Divine Giver.

"In a dream, in a vision of the night, when deep sleep falleth upon men, in slumberings upon the bed; then He openeth the ears of men, and sealeth their instruction." Job 33:15, 16.

When the mind is unoccupied by the cares of waking consciousness, when it is quietly at rest, untroubled by the thoughts that fill it at other times, then the Spirit of God takes full and complete possession, and causes to pass before it the ideas or the images of thought that constitute the divine revelation to be made.

It is, therefore, the characteristic of the gift of prophecy that God makes Himself known to those who have it "in a vision," and "in a dream." This has been the method employed by God in revealing His will, especially to those who received His revelations, and recorded them in the Sacred Word. The terminology of the Bible throughout presupposes the vision-form in the revelations that were made to its writers. The whole body of revelation in the Scripture is presented as a thing seen. Mark the nomenclature of the prophets.

"The vision of Isaiah the son of Amos, *which he*

saw." Isa. 1:1.

The word that Isaiah the son of Amos *saw.*" Isa. 2:1.

"The burden of Babylon, which Isaiah the son of Amos *did see.*" Isa. 13:1.

"The words of Amos, . . . which he saw." Amos 1:1.

"The word of the Lord that came to Micah, . . . *which he saw*." Micah 1:1.

"The burden which Habakkuk the prophet *did see.*" Hab. 1:1.

"The word that the Lord hath *showed* me." Jer. 38:21.

"The prophets have *seen.*" Lam. 2:14.

"The word of the Lord came expressly, . . . and I *looked, and, behold.*" Ezek. 1:3, 4.

"Woe unto the foolish prophets, that follow their own spirit, and *have seen nothing!*" Ezek. 13:3.

"I will watch to *see* what He will say unto me. . . . And the Lord answered me, and said, Write the *vision.*" Hab. 2:1, 2.

It is plain from this language not only that visions and dreams constituted the method of God's revelation to the ancient prophets, but also that the revelations given in this way are not their own but wholly God's. In the employment of this method, the movements of the mind are determined by something outside the subject's will. A power not of himself takes possession of his consciousness and of all his mental processes and controls them in accordance with its own will.

That power is fully recognized and emphatically asserted to be the Spirit of Jehovah.

"And the Spirit of God came upon him, and he prophesied among them." 1 Sam. 10:10.

"Testified against them by Thy Spirit in Thy

prophets." Neh. 9:30.

"The words which the Lord of hosts hath sent in His Spirit by the former prophets." Zech. 7:12.

I will pour out My Spirit upon all flesh; and your sons and your daughters shall prophesy, your old men shall dream dreams, your young men shall see visions." Joel 2:28.

Because it was recognized that it was the Spirit of God that imparted these revelations, a prophet was known as a "man of the Spirit." Hos. 9:7, margin.

Indeed, the very thing that constituted them prophets was that the Spirit was upon them (Isa. 42:1), or poured out upon them (Joel 2:28, 29), and they were as a result filled with the Spirit (Micah 3:8).

In equivalent language "the hand of the Lord," or "the power of the hand" of the Lord, was upon them (2 Kings 3:15; Ezek. 1:3; 3:14, 22; 33:22; 37:1; 40:1), which means they were under divine control.

This control is always complete and compelling. Under it, the prophet becomes the one moved, not the mover, in the formation of his message. This is what Peter means in his wellknown declaration:

"For no prophecy ever came by the will of man: but men spake from God, being moved by the Holy Spirit." 2 Peter. 1:21, A. R. V.

As these messages given through the gift of prophecy are produced by the operation, and determined by the control, of the Spirit of God, the result is raised above anything that could by any possibility be achieved by mere human powers or human wisdom. Its origin, and the Spirit-controlled method of its transmission, constitute it entirely a supernatural product. Human traits are indeed noticeable throughout, but fundamentally it is a divine gift. The most proper mode of speech that can be applied to it is that used by Paul:

"Which things also we speak, not in the words which man's wisdom teacheth, but which the Holy Ghost teacheth." 1 Cor. 2:13.

"The things that I write unto you are the commandments of the Lord." 1 Cor. 14:37.

The instruction given through the gift of prophecy originated in heaven, and is the voice of God to His people. It was given to the church to be heeded and followed, and it came to us under the full direction and control of the Spirit of God. It is a most wonderful privilege to have this gift, and it results in most wonderful blessings to follow its instruction. Divine leadership and divine guidance are the happy lot of the movement that possesses the gift of prophecy.

CHAPTER TWELVE

The Origin of the Testimonies

THE messages, either oral or in writing, that are imparted through the gift of prophecy are known as "testimonies." This is the Scriptural term for them.

This apparently comes from the idea that the prophet is God's mouthpiece, God's spokesman. Therefore he speaks, or witnesses, or *testifies* for God, and what he *testifies* is *testimony.*

So Nehemiah wrote: "Nevertheless they were disobedient, and rebelled against Thee, and cast Thy law behind their backs, and slew Thy prophets *which testified* against them to turn them to Thee." Neh. 9:26.

And again:

"Yet many years didst Thou forbear them, and *testifiedst* against them by Thy Spirit in Thy prophets." Neh. 9:30.

Moses spoke of himself as testifying:

"He said unto them, Set your hearts unto all the words which I *testify* among you this day." Deut. 32:46.

Of the kingdom of Israel it is recorded that "They rejected His statutes, and His covenant that He made with their fathers, and *His testimonies* which *He testified* against them." 2 Kings 17:15.

Nehemiah brought the same charge against Judah:

"Neither have our kings, our princes, our priests, nor our fathers, kept Thy law, nor hearkened unto Thy commandments *and Thy testimonies,* wherewith *Thou didst testify* against them." Neh. 9:34.

There are instances where all that is in the word of God is referred to as "testimony," and the ten-commandment law also. Sometimes, however, as in this passage of Nehemiah, a clear distinction is made between the law, the statutes, the judgments, and the testimonies. Indeed, the prophets are said to give their testimony, or to testify, in order to bring the people to the law of God.

"And *testifiedst* against them, *that Thou mightest bring them again unto Thy law."* Neh. 9:29.

Paul writes that he "testified":

"As we also have forewarned you and *testified."* 1 Thess. 4:6.

His testimony, he declares, was "of God."

"We have testified *of God."* 1 Cor. 15:15.

Again, he says that he testified *in the Lord:*

"Thus I say therefore, *and testify in the Lord."* Eph. 4:17.

Their testimony was not out of their own hearts; it was what they had *seen:*

"We speak that we do know, and *testify that we have seen."* John 3:11.

"And *we have seen* and do *testify."* 1 John 4:14.

In accordance with the true succession of Rev. 1:1, by which truth comes infallibly correct from God to man, so in the Bible God is said to "testify":

"Hear, O My people, and I *will testify* unto thee: O Israel, if thou wilt hearken unto Me." Ps. 81:8.

Jesus testifies:

"He *which testifieth* these things saith, Surely I come quickly." Rev. 22:20.

"I Jesus have sent Mine angel to *testify* unto you these things in the churches." Rev. 22:16.

And John, the representative of those who have the gift of prophecy, also testified.

"For I *testify* unto every man that heareth the words of the prophecy of this book, If any man shall add unto these things, God shall add unto him the plagues that are written in this book." Rev. 22:18.

The "testimonies," or the messages sent through the gift of prophecy, are associated with God's law, and God's statutes, as coming equally from Him; and the Israelites were admonished that their national welfare depended upon heeding God's voice and instruction as contained in them all.

"Ye shall diligently keep the commandments of the Lord your God, and His testimonies, and His statutes, which He hath commanded thee." Deut. 6:17.

The failure to heed this admonition is given as the reason for the destruction which came upon them.

"Ye . . . have not obeyed the voice of the Lord, nor walked in His law, nor in His statutes, nor in *His testimonies;* therefore this evil is happened unto you, as at this day," Jer. 44:23.

It is pointed out again and again in God's word that in heeding His testimonies there is great blessing.

"All the paths of the Lord are mercy and truth unto such as keep His covenant and His testimonies." Ps. 25:10.

The authority and certainty of the testimonies is thus described:

"Thy testimonies are very sure." Ps. 93:5.

The value of the testimonies, and the blessing of

heeding and doing them, together with the counsel and wisdom that come through reading them are set before us in detail in the longest chapter in the Bible, the word *testimonies* being used in this one chapter twenty-three times. Read every passage, and let your soul be deeply impressed by God's estimate of His testimonies.

"Blessed are they that keep His testimonies, and that seek Him with the whole heart." Ps. 119:2.

"I have rejoiced in the way of Thy testimonies, as much as in all riches." Verse 14.

"Remove from me reproach and contempt; for I have kept Thy testimonies." Verse 22.

"Thy testimonies are my delight and my counsellors." Verse 24.

"I have stuck unto Thy testimonies: O Lord, put me not to shame." Verse 32.

"Incline my heart unto Thy testimonies, and not to covetousness." Verse 36.

"I will speak of Thy testimonies also before kings, and will not be ashamed." Verse 46.

"I thought on my ways, and turned my feet unto Thy testimonies." Verse 59.

"Let those that fear Thee turn unto me, and those that have known Thy testimonies." Verse 79.

"Quicken me after Thy lovingkindness; so shall I keep the testimony of Thy mouth." Verse 88.

"The wicked have waited for me to destroy me: but I will consider Thy testimonies." Verse 95.

"I have more understanding than all my teachers: for Thy testimonies are my meditation." Verse 99.

"Thy testimonies have I taken as a heritage for ever: for they are the rejoicing of my heart," Verse 111.

"Thou puttest away all the wicked of the earth like

dross: therefore I love Thy testimonies." Verse 119.

"I am Thy servant; give me understanding, that I may know Thy testimonies." Verse 125.

"Thy testimonies are wonderful: therefore doth my soul keep them." Verse 129.

"Thy testimonies that Thou hast commanded are righteous and very faithful." Verse 138.

"The righteousness of Thy testimonies is everlasting: give me understanding, and I shall live." Verse 144,

"I cried unto Thee; save me, and I shall keep Thy testimonies." Verse 146.

"Concerning Thy testimonies, I have known of old that Thou has founded them for ever." Verse 152.

"Many are my persecutors and mine enemies; yet do I not decline from Thy testimonies" Verse 157.

"My soul hath kept Thy testimonies; and I love them exceedingly." Verse 167.

"I have kept Thy precepts and Thy testimonies: for all my ways are before Thee." Verse 168.

CHAPTER THIRTEEN

Seer, Messenger, Prophet, Watch-man, Spokesman

THOSE to whom God has given the gift of prophecy are properly called prophets. This, however, is not the only word used in the Scriptures to describe their work and office.

Because it was in the form of visions that they obtained their instruction, the prophets were sometimes called "seers."

"Beforetime in Israel, when a man went to inquire of God, thus he spake, Come, and let us go to the *seer*: for he that is now called a *Prophet* was beforetime called a *Seer*." 1 Sam. 9:9.

We have already discussed the seeing powers of the gift of prophecy, and emphasized the fact that the instruction given through this gift was shown to the prophet, and therefore come from outside himself. He not only *saw* what God showed him, but in the light of what he had been shown he then *saw* the world, men, society, the human heart, with clearer and truer vision than others.

Those who possess the gift of prophecy are also spoken of in the Bible as "messengers."

"And the Lord God of their fathers sent to them by His messengers." 2 Chron. 36:15.

That "prophets" and "messengers" are the same is apparent from two passages:

"Came the word of the Lord by *Haggai the prophet.*" Haggai 1:1.

"Then spake *Haggai the Lord's messenger* in the Lord's message unto the people." Haggai 1:13.

Of John the Baptist, also, it is written:

"But what went ye out for to see? A *prophet?* Yea, I say unto you, and much more than a *prophet.* This is he, of whom it is written, Behold, I send My *messenger* before Thy face, which shall prepare Thy way before Thee. For I say unto you, Among those that are born of women there is no greater *prophet* than John the Baptist." Luke 7:26-28.

Of Ezekiel, who declares that "the heavens were opened, and I saw visions of God" (Ezek. 1:1), it is recorded, "Son of man, I have made thee a watchman unto the house of Israel: therefore hear the word at My mouth, and give them warning from Me." Ezek. 3:17.

The duties of a watchman are clear. A heavy responsibility rests upon him. In times of public danger he is set apart to warn the city of approaching danger. Trusting him, the people go about their ordinary occupations unafraid and in security so long as he does not sound his trumpet. If he should sleep at his post, or neglect to warn of danger, men are caught unprepared, and lives are lost through his fault. And their blood is required at his hand. If, however, he faithfully sounds the alarm when danger comes, and men disregard his warning and are cut down in their iniquity, their blood is upon their own heads.

Such, as prophet, was Ezekiel's position and work. The prophet, then, is one who sees further into the spiritual issues of things than other men, enlightened as he is by God, and who sees also the coming calamity that to others is invisible. Thus seeing, the prophet's duty and course are clear. His business is to announce as in trumpet tones the doom hanging over men, and point out the way of escape.

In carrying out this prophetic duty, the prophet does not confine himself to predicting the future. That is a most limited view of the prophetic work, and only a part of it.

On the basis of what he has been shown God is about to do in the future, the prophet proclaims and preaches religious truth. In other words, he proclaims new truth, or restates old truth, in the light and setting of what he sees God is soon to do, and which he is inspired to foresee and to interpret. His business is not all foreseeing nor all teaching. It is teaching grounded upon foresight.

How extensively a prophet may deal with all the truth of God in carrying out the duties of his prophetic office may be seen from the study of only one of the chapters of Ezekiel, the 18th. Here the prophet sets forth the exact and absolute righteousness of God; the unwillingness of God that any should perish; the desire of God for all to be saved and live; the necessity of personal repentance; and the freedom and independence of the individual soul in its relation to God.

The broadest and most general description of the work of a prophet that the Scriptures contain is that foretelling the prophetic office of our Lord Himself.

"I will raise them up a Prophet from among their brethren, like unto thee, and *will put My words in his mouth; and He shall speak unto them all that I shall command Him.*" Deut. 18:18.

A seer, a prophet, a messenger, a watchman. These

words convey the true idea of the work of one who has the gift of prophecy. Some understand the word "prophet" in far too limited a sense. They restrict its meaning to the one function of predicting the future. This is a mistake. The gift of prophecy deals with far more than the future. The past and the, present are as much a part of its province as the future, and its revealed instruction throws great light upon them.

The apostle John, in preparing the book of Revelation, was instructed to "write the things which thou *hast seen,* and the things which *are,* and the things which *shall be hereafter." Rev.* 1:19.

There it is,—past, present, and future are covered in the divine illumination which is given through the gift of prophecy. On this point, Dr. A. Plummer, in his book, "The Pastoral Epistles," says this:

"If we may venture to coin words in order to bring out points of differences, there are three main ideas involved in the title 'prophet.' (1) A *for*-teller; one who speaks *for* or instead of another, especially one who speaks *for* or in the name of God; a divine messenger, ambassador, interpreter, or *spokesman.* (2) A *forth*-teller; one who has a special message to deliver *forth* to the world; a proclaimer, harbinger, or herald. (3) A *fore*-teller; one who tells *beforehand* what is coming; a predicter of future events. To be the bearer or interpreter of a divine message is the fundamental conception of the prophet in classical Greek; and to a large extent this conception prevails in both the Old and the New Testament. To be in immediate intercourse with Jehovah, and to be His spokesman to Israel, was what the Hebrews understood by the gift of prophecy. It was by no means necessary that the divine communication which the prophet had to make known to the people should relate to the future. It might be a denunciation of past sins, or an exhortation respecting present conduct, quite as naturally as a prediction of what was coming. And in the Acts and Pauline Epistles the idea of a prophet remains much the same. He is one to whom has been granted special insight into God's counsels, and who communicates these mysteries to others. Both in the Jewish and primitive Christian dispensations, the prophets are the means of communication between God and His Church. Eight persons are mentioned by name in the Acts of the Apostles as exercising this gift of prophecy: Agabus, Barnabas, Symeon called Niger, Lucius of Cyrene, Manaen the foster brother of Herod the tetrarch, Judas, Silas, and the apostle Paul. On certain occasions the divine communications made to them by the Spirit included a knowledge of the future; as when Agabus foretold the great famine (Acts 11:28) and the imprisonment of St. Paul (21:11), and when St. Paul told that the Holy Spirit testified to him in every city, that bonds and afflictions awaited him. (20:23). But this is the exception rather than the rule. It is in their character of prophets that Judas and Silas exhort and confirm the brethren."—"*The Pastoral Epistles,*" pp. 65, 66.

Prophets, then, are not, as some have seemed to think, miraculous conjurers, whose principal business is solving perplexing puzzles, finding lost articles, and making astounding revelations, all of which have been hidden from others. The object of their messages is always quite practical. As prophets of God they necessarily deal with eternal truth, especially that truth which belongs in a peculiar way to their own times. They are not mere opportunists. Their strength and power are in their grasp of fundamental principles. This is why the messages of the ancient prophets still live, and are of lasting use to the church in every age. And this is why the messages of the spirit of prophecy today are of such vital importance and large benefit to the life and work and progress of the church today.

CHAPTER FOURTEEN

Counterfeiting the Prophetic Gift

As in all ages God has had His agents for the teaching of truth, so in all ages Satan has sent forth his agents to teach error and to deceive. As there have been true prophets, so there have been false prophets. As God has used the true gift of prophecy, so Satan has imitated it and used a false gift of prophecy.

Satan has a religion of his own. Sacrifice is a part of it.

"They shall no more offer their sacrifices unto devils." Lev. 17:7.

"The things which the Gentiles sacrifice, they sacrifice to devils, and not to God: and I would not that ye should have fellowship with devils." 1 Cor. 10:20.

Satan has a system of worship, a body of teaching, a priesthood, or ministry. He has a spirit by which he controls his agents, working miracles, giving dreams and revelations, in imitation of the divine gift of prophecy.

"Wherein in time past ye walked according to the course of this world, according to the prince of the power of the air, *the spirit* that now worketh in the children of disobedience." Eph. 2:2.

"They are the *spirits of devils, working miracles,* which go forth unto the kings of the earth and of the whole world, to gather them to the battle of that great day of God Almighty." Rev. 16:14.

The agents of Satan on earth in his work of deception, that is, his prophets, are called diviners, dreamers, enchanters, sorcerers, witches, charmers, astrologers, magicians, spirit-mediums, wizards, and necromancers.

"There shall not be found among you anyone that maketh his son or his daughter to pass through the fire, or that useth divination, or an observer of times, or an enchanter, or a witch, or a charmer, or a consulter with familiar spirits, or a wizard, or a necromancer. For all that do these things are an abomination unto the Lord." Deut. 18:10-12.

Here is a list of eight different classes of those who dealt in occult and forbidden mysteries.

First there is the diviner, or one who sought a knowledge of future events and hidden things by means of arrows or rods, by images, and by inspecting the entrails of freshly killed animals. (Ezek. 21:21.)

The observer of times is literally, as the Vulgate has its, an *observer of dreams and omens.* This is soothsaying, by which information was obtained by relying on dreams and revelations. It was common in Assyria, Egypt, Philistia, and apostate Israel. (2 Kings 21:6; 2 Chron. 33:6; Isa. 2:6; Micah 5:12.)

Enchanting covered serpent-charming and, as was the custom of the Roman augurs, the observance of omens and signs and the singing and flight of birds, in an effort thus to find out the secrets of the occult and mysterious.

A witch or sorcerer was one who practiced

divination by prayers to demons, and by administering drugs, such as love and hatred philters, as well as obtaining information by means of a familiar spirit.

A charmer was one who by the use of song, amulets, magnetism, charms, hypnotism, and demoniacal powers bound evil spells upon men, and thus sought to obtain desired objects and information.

A consulter with familiar spirits was one who had made a compact with an invisible intelligence, pretending to be the spirit of a dead person, and who called up these spirits and consulted them in order to obtain oracular answers. Today they are called spirit mediums.

A wizard was a wise man, a magician, one who by his own mental power, and with the aid of occult art, gained information from secret sources and thus obtained the name of possessing supernatural wisdom.

The necromancer was also one who consulted with spirits, who claimed to evoke the spirits of the dead and obtain from them answers to such queries as he put to them.

Other agents of Satan in deceiving mankind are mentioned in Isaiah 47:13 by the names of "astrologers," "stargazers," and "monthly prognosticators."

The occult practices covered in these passages were accompanied by the basest and vilest immoralities and licentiousness, as well as by cruelty and barbarism. It is because of their connection with Satan, their inspiration by Satan, and their unspeakable vileness and cruelty, that "all that do these things are an abomination unto the Lord."

And all who engage in them today are equally abominable in His sight.

Satan even goes so far as to imitate the method by

which God imparts instruction through the genuine gift of prophecy, that is, visions and dreams.

"They have *seen vanity and lying divination*. . . . Have ye not seen a *vain* vision, and have ye not spoken *a lying divination.*" Ezek. 13:6, 7.

"Her prophets have daubed them with untempered mortar, *seeing vanity, and divining lies* unto them." Ezek. 22:28.

"I have heard what the prophets said, that prophesy lies in My name, saying, *I have dreamed, I have dreamed.* . . . Which think to cause My people to forget My name by their *dreams.* . . . Behold I am against them that prophesy *false dreams,* saith the Lord, and do tell them, and cause My people to err by their lies, and by their lightness; yet I sent them not nor commanded them." Jer. 23:25, 27, 32.

Satanic spirits, pretending to be the spirits of the dead, are the agents who convey information to these false prophets. Deut. 18:10-12; 1 Sam. 28:8-16; Rev. 16:13, 14.

This Satanic, miracle-working power, manifesting itself through false prophets, is to be a special sign in these last days, just before the second coming of our Lord. God's people are especially warned against these false prophets.

"There shall arise false Christs, and false prophets, and shall show great signs and wonders; insomuch that, if it were possible, they shall deceive the very elect. Behold I have told you before." Matt. 24:24, 25.

It is certain that God will manifest the true gift of prophecy in connection with the final movement of the gospel, and make it the possession of His remnant church.

It is also certain that Satan will, with mighty

power and signs, manifest the false gifts of prophecy and send false prophets into the world.

The Bible bids us to "despise not prophesyings." It also warns us to beware of false prophets. (1 Thess. 5:20; Matt. 7:15.)

These admonitions and warnings would be of no particular service to us if there were no way to determine the true from the false, and detect the counterfeit.

It is plain, therefore, that there must be some method disclosed in God's work by which the gift of prophecy may be tested, and the true established, and the false exposed.

We must now study what these tests are.

CHAPTER FIFTEEN

Bible Tests of the Gift of Prophecy

THERE is danger for the people of God today from false prophets. Their purpose, or Satan's purpose who uses them, is to perform such signs and wonders as will deceive, if possible, the very elect.

We turn, therefore, with quickened interest to a consideration of the ways and means by which the true gift of prophecy may be determined from the false.

Nor need we fear that we are encroaching on the forbidden when we apply these tests to the gift of prophecy, whether true or false. On the contrary God has not only commanded us to make such tests, but also laid down the very principles upon which the tests shall be made.

It is because false prophets are engaged in their work of deception that we are bidden to test them.

"Beloved, believe not every spirit, but try the spirits whether they are of God: *because* many false prophets are gone out into the world." 1 John 4:1.

God would not command us to try the spirits of the prophets without providing for us the rules and standards by which they should be tested. These we will find in His word. Let us study some of them. Here is one rule:

"*Hereby know ye* the Spirit of God: *Every spirit that confesseth that Jesus Christ is come in the flesh is of God: and every spirit that confesseth not that Jesus Christ is come in the flesh is not of God*: and this is that spirit of antichrist." 1 John 4:2, 3.

Here is the essential test, fidelity to the central facts and truths of the atonement of Christ. Christ must be acknowledged, honored, worshiped, and upheld. There must be loyalty to all that He taught, all that He did, all that He is, all that He is to do. The whole tendency of the life, the work, the teaching, of the gift of prophecy must be to exalt Him, glorify Him, and lead men to Him. This is fundamental. If there is any failure here, no matter what other credentials the prophet may have or show, no matter what miracles he may work, no matter what signs he may show, he is a false prophet, and belongs to Satan, if he is not true to the historic Christ and historic Christianity. Loyalty to the person of Christ, to His pre-existence, His divine incarnation, His deity, His divine Sonship, His virgin birth, His miracle-working power, the divine authority of His teaching, His substitutionary and expiatory death, His literal resurrection, His ascension, His mediatory and intercessory priesthood, and the promise of His bodily, visible, personal, and imminent return—this is the fundamental test as to whether a prophet is false or true.

Agreeing with this is the test urge upon us in Isaiah.

When they shall say unto you, Seek unto them that have familiar spirits, and unto wizards that peep, and that mutter: should not a people seek unto their God?

for the living to the dead? *To the law and to the testimony: if they speak not according to this word,* it is because there is no light in them." Isa. 8:19, 20.

In each of these suggested trials the ultimate test of prophecy is to be the fundamental principles of the faith. Any statement made by one who pretends to possess the gift of prophecy that is contrary to the word of God is to be sufficient to stamp that prophet as false. The gift of prophecy is not to test the Bible; the Bible is to test the gift of prophecy. "If they speak not according to *this word,* it is because there is no light in them."

The Bible gives us an illustration as to how this test is to be applied. In the 28th chapter of Jeremiah there is recorded a conflict between Jeremiah, the prophet of God, and Hananiah, a false prophet. Just before this the king of Babylon had carried away Jeconiah the king of Judah, with the treasures of the temple and the strongest of the people. Jeremiah had declared that they should not be returned. He had gone further than this, and foretold additional calamity, predicting that Nebuchadnezzar would come again and would take away the remaining vessels of the temple and the remaining people.

Hananiah, in opposition to this, declared, as coming from Jehovah, that "within two full years will I bring again into this place all the vessels of the Lord's house, that Nebuchadnezzar king of Babylon took away from this place. . . . I will bring again to this place Jeconiah . . . with all the captives of Judah," Jer. 28:3, 4.

Jeremiah's conduct under these circumstances is striking and significant. He did not at once denounce his rival as a false prophet. He may have thought

Hananiah might possibly have a true word from Jehovah, since, as is clear in the book of Jonah, the most positive prophecies were conditional, and perhaps repentance on the part of the people might bring upon the nation a blessing instead of the evil he had foreseen. Consequently Jeremiah expresses a fervent wish that Hananiah's prophecy might come true. But in doing so he applies the ultimate test of prophecy. These are his words:

"Jeremiah said, Amen: the Lord do so: the Lord perform thy words which thou has prophesied, to bring again the vessels of the Lord's house, and all that is carried away captive, from Babylon unto this place. Nevertheless hear thou now this word that I speak in thine ears, and in the ears of all the people; *the prophets that have been before me and before thee of old* prophesied both against many countries, and against great kingdoms, of war, and of evil, and of pestilence. The prophet which prophesieth of peace, when the word of the prophet shall come to pass, then shall the prophet be known, that the Lord hath truly sent him." Jer. 28:6-9.

After this, while the people, and perhaps even Jeremiah, were in perplexity, definite revelation was made to Jeremiah that Hananiah was a false prophet. Jeremiah did not hesitate then to denounce him.

"Then said the prophet Jeremiah unto Hananiah the prophet, Hear now, Hananiah; The Lord hath not sent thee; but thou makest this people to trust in a lie. Therefore thus saith the Lord; Behold, I will cast thee from off the face of the earth: this year thou shalt die, because thou hast taught rebellion against the Lord. So Hananiah the prophet died the same year in the seventh month." Jer. 28:15-17.

The whole narrative is not only interesting and illuminating, but is of extreme importance. It shows us how the prophets themselves regarded their own supernatural powers, and how they tested the false gift of prophecy. This they did by asking at outset how the new word of Jehovah compared with the older words, which there was no doubt He had spoken, how the present word stood in regard to the words of "the prophets that have been before me and before thee of old."

If any possible way appeared by which the new could be reconciled to the old, the new might be given the benefit of the doubt, and left to the decision of the event. If Jeremiah had seen at once that Hananiah's prediction was wholly contrary to some former prophecy, he undoubtedly would have denounced him at once under the law of Deut. 13:1-5. As it was, however, he waited, and no doubt would have continued to wait in an attitude of watchful neutrality, had not Jehovah himself settled the question by an additional revelation.

There is another test that Jeremiah carried out in this case that also is given to us by definite instruction in the Bible. He proposed that the event foretold, whether it came to pass or failed of fulfillment, should determine the origin of the prophecy. This is in accord with the Scripture.

"The prophet which shall presume to speak a word in My name, which I have not commanded him to speak, or that shall speak in the name of other gods, even that prophet shall die. And if thou say in thy heart, How shall we know the word which the Lord hath not spoken? When a prophet speaketh in the name of the Lord, *if the thing follow not, nor come to pass, that is the thing which the Lord hath not spoken,* but the prophet hath spoken it presumptuously: thou shalt not be afraid of him." Deut. 18:20-22.

False predictions expose themselves by the non-occurence of the event foretold. When a prophet's words enter the realm of the future, his predictions must not fail of fulfillment if he is to be considered as a true prophet of God.

These are the tests of great importance in connection with the gift of prophecy. There are others of a physical character which will be mentioned later, but these are fundamental and decisive.

"To the law and to the testimony: if they speak not according to this word, it is because there is no light in them." Isa. 8:20.
"When the word of the prophet shall come to pass, then shall the prophet be known, that the Lord hath truly sent him." Jer. 28:9.

CHAPTER SIXTEEN

Testing the Prophetic Gift

EXAMINED by the tests that the word of God proposes, all prophets, all who speak in God's name, all who claim to possess the gift of prophecy, can be successfully and decisively tried, and proved false or true.

If they are from God, they will glorify and exalt Christ as the Saviour of the world, they will speak in accordance with every teaching of His Holy Word, and their predictions will meet an exact fulfillment.

Those, therefore, who pretend to receive communications from the dead, such as spirit mediums and clairvoyants, are false prophets, doing the work of Satan. For the dead know not anything, are without consciousness, and God has forbidden pretended consultation with them.

"The dead know not anything." Eccl. 9:5.

"There shall not be found among you any one that [is] a consulter with familiar spirits, . . . for all that do these things are an abomination unto the Lord." Deut. 18:10-12.

All who teach disobedience to God's law are false prophets. (Deut. 13:1-5.)

"To the law and to the testimony: if they speak not according to this word, it is because there is no light in them." Isa. 8:20.

All who speak against the Sabbath of the Lord are false prophets.

"There is a conspiracy of her prophets in the midst thereof, . . . they have devoured souls; . . . and have profaned mine holy things; they have put no difference between the holy and profane, . . . and have hid their eyes from My Sabbaths; and I am profaned among them. . . . And her prophets have daubed them with untempered mortar, seeing vanity, and divining lies unto them, saying, Thus saith the Lord God, when the Lord hath not spoken." Ezek. 22:25-28.

All who deny the incarnation of Christ, that He came in the flesh, are most assuredly false prophets. (1 John 4:1-3.)

All who claim divine inspiration for themselves but deny the inspiration of the Bible are false prophets.

"All Scripture is given by inspiration of God, and is profitable for doctrine, for reproof, for correction, for instruction in righteousness: that the man of God may be perfect, throughly furnished unto all good works." 2 Tim. 3:16, 17.

"For the prophecy came not in old time by the will of man: but holy men of God spake as they were moved by the Holy Ghost." 2 Pet. 1:21.

"For I testify unto every man that heareth the words of the prophecy of this book, If any man shall add unto these things, God shall add unto him the plagues that are written in this book: and if any man shall take away from the words of the book of this prophecy, God shall take away his part out of the book of life, and out of the holy city, and from the things which are written in this book." Rev. 22:18, 19.

All who pretend to speak for God and yet whose
lives are unholy and impure are false prophets.

"Behold, ye trust in lying words, that cannot
profit. Will ye steal, murder, and commit adultery, and
swear falsely, and burn incense unto Baal, and walk
after other gods whom ye know not; and come and
stand before me in this house, which is called by My
name, and say, We are delivered to do all these abomi-
nations? "Jer. 7:8-10.

"I have seen also in the prophets of Jerusalem an
horrible thing: they commit adultery, and walk in lies:
they strengthen also the hands of evildoers, that none
doth turn from his wickedness: they are all of them
unto Me as Sodom, and the inhabitants thereof as
Gomorrah." Jer. 23:14.

True prophets, who are really sent of God, and
who have the genuine gift of prophecy, will be in
harmony in all that they do and say with the teachings
of the Bible, with all that the former prophets have
taught.

True prophets will be in harmony with the law of
God.

"[Thou] testifiedst against them, that Thou
mightest bring them again unto Thy law: yet they
dealt proudly, and hearkened not unto Thy commandments, . . . yet many years didst Thou forbear them,
and testifiedst against them by Thy Spirit in Thy
prophets." Neh. 9:29, 30.

"To the *law* and to the testimony: if they speak not
according to this word." Isa. 8:20.

True prophets will be in harmony, as were the
ancient prophets, with the Sabbath of Jehovah.

"Blessed is the man that doeth this, and the son of
man that layeth hold on it; that keepeth the Sabbath

from polluting it, and keepeth his hand from doing any evil." Isa. 56:2.

The ancient prophets urged the people to observe the Sabbath of the Lord, and rebuked them for its desecration. (Ezek. 20:12-20; Neh. 13:15-21.)

True prophets will exalt Jesus Christ as the Saviour of the world, and the whole tendency of their lives, their acts, their words, will be to influence men towards Him. (1 John 4:1-3.).

True prophets will be in harmony with all the former prophets have written, and will direct men to the writings of the former prophets as the foundation of truth.

"Abraham saith unto him, They have Moses and the prophets; let them hear them. . . . If they hear not Moses and the prophets, neither will they be persuaded, though one rose from the dead." Luke 16:29, 31.

"Beginning at Moses and all the prophets, He expounded unto them in all the Scriptures the things concerning Himself. . . . And He said unto them, These are the words which I spake unto you, while I was yet with you, that all things must be fulfilled, which were written in the law of Moses, and in the prophets, and in the Psalms, concerning Me. Then opened He their understanding, that they might understand the Scriptures." Luke 24:27, 44, 45.

That is an example of the attitude of the true gift of prophecy towards the Scriptures.

"But this I confess unto thee, that after the way which they call heresy, so worship I the God of my fathers, believing all things which are written in the law and in the prophets." Acts 24:14.

"Saying none other things than those which the

prophets and Moses did say should come: that Christ should suffer, and that He should be the first that should rise from the dead, and should show light unto the people, and to the Gentiles." Acts 26:22, 23.

True prophets will lead holy, upright, consistent lives, which will influence men for good. It was "*holy men of God*" who were moved by the Holy Ghost to produce the ancient prophecies. The prophet's life will witness to his having been with God and learned of Him.

"Every tree that bringeth not forth good fruit is hewn down, and cast into the fire. Wherefore by their fruits ye, shall know them." Matt. 7:19, 20.

CHAPTER SEVENTEEN

Physical Tests of the Prophetic Gift

IN addition to the primary tests of the gift of prophecy already noticed, there are others of a physical nature that seem to be of some importance, as the Spirit of God has taken some pains to describe them when telling of the condition of prophets in vision. Some of these tests are of such a nature that neither false prophets, nor even Satan, the inspirer of false prophets, can imitate or counterfeit them.

When "the Spirit of God came upon" Balaam, "he took up his parable, and said, Balaam the son of Beor hath said, and the man whose *eyes are open* hath said: he hath said, which heard the words of God, which *saw the vision of the Almighty, falling into a trance, but having his eyes open.*" Num. 24:2-4.

As if this emphasis and repetition were not sufficient to direct the desired attention to this physical phenomenon, it is gone over again:

"And he took up his parable, and said, Balaam the son of Boor hath said, and the man whose *eyes are open* hath said: he hath said, which heard the words of God, and knew the knowledge of the most High, which *saw the vision of the Almighty, falling into a trance, but having his eyes open.*" Verses 15, 16.

Why this emphasis and reiteration regarding the open eyes? Apparently the Spirit desires us to note this as a condition to be looked for when a true vision is being given the one who has the gift of prophecy.

This open condition of the eyes is also implied in the terminology used by the prophets regarding the manner of their receiving their visions. Notice their language:

"The vision of Isaiah, . . . which he *saw*." Isa. 1:1.

"The word that Isaiah . . . *saw*." Isa 2:1.

"The burden of Babylon, which Isaiah . . . *did see*." Isa. 13:1.

"The word that the Lord hath *showed* me." Jer. 38:21.

"The word of the Lord came, . . . and I *looked*, and, *behold*." Ezek. 1:3, 4.

"*I saw* in my vision." Dan. 7:2.

"Then I *lifted up mine eyes, and looked,*" Dan. 10:5.

"The words of Amos, . . . which he *saw*." Amos 1:1.

"The burden which Habakkuk . . . *did see*." Hab. 1:1.

"And I *saw* the seven angels." Rev. 8:2.

"And I *looked,* and, lo, a Lamb stood on mount Sion." Rev. 14:1.

All of which implies eyes that are *open*.

The condition of the prophet Daniel while in holy vision is described in much detail. The Spirit of God does not waste words in writing the Scripture. Every word has a purpose. The details of this trancelike condition of the prophet would not have been included in the Bible if they were not important. In these things God is evidently giving us instruction regarding the condition of all true prophets in vision.

We do well to heed it.

"I Daniel alone saw the vision: for the men that, were with me saw not the vision; but a great quaking fell upon them, so that they fled to hide themselves. Therefore I was left alone, and saw this great vision, *and there remained no strength in me:* for my comeliness was turned in me into corruption, and *I retained no strength.* Yet heard I the voice of his words: and when I heard the voice of his words, then was I in a deep sleep on my face, and my face toward the ground. . . .

"And when he had spoken such words unto me, I set my face toward the ground, and I became dumb. And, behold, one like the similitude of the sons of men touched my lips: then I opened my mouth, and spake, and said unto him that stood before me, O my lord, by the vision my sorrows are turned upon me, and *I have retained no strength.* For how can the servant of this my lord talk with this my lord? For as for me, straightway *there remaineth no strength in me, neither is there breath left in me.* Then there came again and touched me one like the appearance of a man, and he *strengthened me,* and said, O man greatly beloved, fear not: peace be unto thee, be strong, yea, be strong. And when he had spoken unto me, *I was strengthened,* and said, Let my lord speak; for *thou hast strengthened me.*" Dan. 10:7-9, 15-19.

First, there is a condition of utter and complete weakness, even exhaustion. "There remained no strength in me." John on Patmos, was affected in a very similar way. "And when I saw Him, I fell at His feet as dead." Rev. 1:17. They stood in the presence of God, they saw visions of the divine character and glory, they beheld God's purposes unfold in future events, they saw God, and heaven, and eternal realities. It was too much for them. Their physical powers could not sustain them. They were prostrated, and sank from exhaustion.

While Daniel was in this trancelike condition, the angel spoke; and Daniel listened and heard. When the angel touched his lips, indicating that he could speak, he called attention to his condition. Then the angel not only told him to "be strong, yea, be strong," but imparted supernatural strength to him. This was not the restoration of his own natural powers, but the conferring upon him of a supernatural strength.

And during all this time he had no *breath,* and was not *breathing.* "Neither is there breath left in me"—a condition beyond Satan's power to imitate.

Very modestly Paul describes his own experience while in vision and receiving revelations from God.

"I will come to visions and revelations of the Lord. I knew a man in Christ above fourteen years ago, (whether in the body, I cannot tell; or whether out of the body, I cannot tell: God knoweth;) such an one caught up to the third heaven. And I knew such a man, (whether in the body, or out of the body, I cannot tell: God knoweth;) how that he was caught up into paradise, and heard unspeakable words, which it is not lawful for a man to utter." 2 Cor. 12:1-4.

Here an additional item in the description of a true prophet in vision is given. He was in a state of insensibility regarding his earthly surroundings, totally unconscious as to what was going on about him. God had taken such complete control of his mental and intellectual faculties, and they were so concentrated upon and absorbed in the contemplation of the heavenly scenes passing before him, that he was as one dead to all surrounding occurrences. He was so altogether unconscious of the world as to be entirely removed from it. He was in the third heaven, in paradise.

Physical tests of a person in true vision are therefore to be found in these five things: utter weakness at first, open eyes throughout, bodily functions and life itself maintained without breath, complete unconsciousness of surroundings, and impartation of supernatural strength. These conditions will characterize the receiving of a revelation from God through the genuine gift of prophecy.

One of these tests cannot be imitated by men. The true prophet in vision does not breathe. This condition may continue for a long time, half an hour, an hour, two hours. A person pretending to have the gift of prophecy could not meet such a test. Without divine aid life cannot be maintained without breathing.

Putting these physical tests with the others already discussed, it is clear that God has made it possible for His people to distinguish between the true and the false gift of prophecy. They are safeguarded against being led astray if they will carefully apply these tests, as they are bidden to do.

"The man whose eyes are open hath said: he hath said, which heard the words of God, and knew the knowledge of the most High, which saw the vision of the Almighty, falling into a trance, but having his eyes open." Num. 24:15, 16.

CHAPTER EIGHTEEN

The Prophetic Gift Restored

T HE gift of prophecy has been restored. Fulfilling the prophecy of Rev. 12:17, this important gift, unknown for long centuries during the apostasy in the church, has been manifested again among the people of God. As foretold in the prophecy, it has been given to the "remnant" church, the church that keep "the commandments of God," and, consequently "have the testimony of Jesus," which is, "the spirit of prophecy." (Rev. 19:10.)

The gift of prophecy was known and manifested in the Christian church at the beginning, in the days of the apostles. We know from the prophetic word (Rev. 12:17) that it is again to be known and manifested in God's true church, His commandment-keeping church, in the time of the end. It was removed from the church because of apostasy. When men departed from God, especially when they cast his law behind their backs, and displaced and disregarded His sabbath, substituting a false and counterfeit sabbath in its place, He took from them this gift.

The light of truth was not, however, always to be obscured by the darkness of error. The time was to come when the falsehoods were to be exposed and the church called back to its former allegiance and purity of faith. The Reformation began the work, but did not proceed far enough to restore the Sabbath to its rightful place. This was to be done in the final movement and message of the gospel on earth.

Our attention is directed by the prophecy of Daniel to the end of the 2300 years (Dan. 8:14) as the time when the final message would begin—a message that would again set before the whole earth those truths which had been hidden for so long by the errors of the apostasy.

The 2300 years began in 457 B.C. They ended in 1844 A.D. It is to that time the prophecy directs our attention. At that time a work was to begin in heaven called the cleansing of the sanctuary. At that same time a message of truth was to begin on earth that would restore every lost and perverted truth of the gospel. These two were to go forward together until Jesus came again: the work of Christ in heaven in the most holy place, and the work of His church on earth, that of proclaiming His message, of truth.

To bear this message to the world it was necessary for God to raise up a new movement and people, separate from the established churches, for they had refused to walk in the advancing light, and had rejected the Sabbath truth. The message now to be given to the world is the threefold message predicted in Revelation: "And I saw another angel fly in the midst of heaven, having the everlasting gospel to preach unto them that dwell on the earth, and to every nation, and kindred, and tongue, and people, saying with a loud voice, Fear God, and give glory to Him; for the hour of His judgment is come: and worship Him that made heaven, and earth, and the sea, and the fountains of waters. And there followed another angel, saying, Babylon is fallen, is fallen, that great city, because she made all nations drink of the wine of the wrath of her fornication. And the third angel followed them, saying with a loud voice, If any man worship the beast and his image, and receive his mark in his forehead, or in his hand, the same shall drink of the wine of the wrath of God, which is poured out without mixture into the cup of his indignation; and he shall be tormented with fire and brimstone in the presence of the holy angels, and in the presence of the Lamb; and the smoke of their torment ascendeth up for ever and ever: and they have no rest day nor night, who worship the beast and his image, and whosoever receiveth the mark of his name. Here is the patience of the saints: here are they that keep the commandments of God, and the faith of Jesus. And I heard a voice from heaven saying unto me, Write, Blessed are the dead which die in the Lord from henceforth: yea, saith the Spirit, that they may rest from their labors; and their works do follow them. And I looked, and behold a white cloud, and upon the cloud One sat like unto the Son of man, having on His head a golden crown, and in His hand a sharp sickle." Rev. 14:6-14.

The characteristics of this special, threefold, last-day message are worthy of special attention. They are these: It brings back in its purity and power the primitive, eternal good news of the gospel; it bears a message to every nation, kindred, tongue, and people; it calls men back to the fear (or reverence and worship) of the Creator, which is the beginning of wisdom; it announces the hour of God's judgment as already come; it calls attention to the fall of creed-bound churches; it warns against the worship of the beast and his image in contrast with the worship of the

Creator; it tells men what to do as well as what not to do; it restores obedience to "the commandments of God"; it teaches the very "faith of Jesus"; it tells men how to obtain the victory; it preaches the second coming of our Lord; and it makes ready a people prepared for the Lord.

This message, then, fits the present situation. It is a message given for this particular time and to meet the special conditions that prevail on the earth today.

This final message of the gospel of Christ will so fully prepare those who receive it to meet God that they are said to be without fault before His throne. (Revelation 14:5.) It is therefore evident that the message borne by the third angel will contain all the truth of God. It is through the truth (John 17:17) that the people of God are sanctified; and if those who accept the third angel's message became without fault before the throne of God, it will be because they have the full and complete truth of the gospel.

"This gospel of the kingdom," the message of the coming kingdom, will also "be preached in all the world for a witness unto all nations [not that all will be converted, but "for a witness"] and then shall the end come" (Matt. 24:14). That is, a people will be raised up, as was John the Baptist, who will take the message of the coming Saviour and the fullness of the truth of His gospel to all the world before His second coming. And when they have completed this task— when they have warned the world, and given it the truth, and the world has rejected the message—"then shall the end come." To this people, bearing this message, the gift of prophecy will be restored.

CHAPTER NINETEEN

The Closing Work of the Gospel

ALL lost truths of the gospel are to be recovered. All truths that have been perverted are to be restored. All hidden truths are to be brought to the light. The gospel in its primitive fullness and simplicity is to be preached to the world again. The deceptions, the delusions, the errors, that have gained an entrance into the body of Christian teaching are to be cast out. The truth of the Lord Jesus in all its glory and power is to be presented to the world in the final gospel message.

This message had its beginning in 1844, at the close of the 2300 years of Daniel 8:14. The very heart and center of it is Jesus, our great High Priest. He is in the message restored to His rightful place as "the way, the truth, and the life." The attention of the, world is to be directed to His expiatory, propitiatory, and mediatorial work.

The movement that God institutes to carry His final message to the world will emphasize the fundamental truths of the gospel. It will turn away from all the perversions of truth, from all the errors that men have brought in, and point alone to Jesus as the author and finisher of faith. It will maintain the historic faith, the apostolic faith of the Christian church, and make the person of our Lord the central feature of its teaching.

It will emphasize His pre-existence as the divine Creator. It will uphold the Scriptural record of His virgin birth. It will present the truth of His divine Sonship. It will insist on His authority as the Teacher sent from God. It will defend His miracle-working power. It will cherish His enduring words. It will maintain the essential truth of His substitutionary death. It will hold to the certainty of His miraculous resurrection and ascension. It will understand and teach His divine intercession and priesthood. And it will confidently look for His literal, bodily, imminent return.

This last church, which will be the full fruitage of the Reformation, will have revealed to it all the truths of the gospel, the truths that Satan has so successfully hidden under the great counterfeit system during the centuries of the Dark Ages. It will, therefore, preach not only the message that the Lord is soon to come, but it will also possess and teach the truth concerning the true God, the true Saviour, the true sanctuary, the true priesthood, the true law, the true Sabbath, and those other truths which have been perverted. It is to this church, the remnant church, that the gift of prophecy will be restored.

The people, then, who will deliver the final message of the gospel to the world will believe in God the Father as the great King of the universe. They will believe in His infinite love for all His creatures, and in His great plan for the salvation of sinners.

They will believe in and preach Christ as the only Saviour from sin. They will present Him to the world as the great Sin-bearer for the human race, and will show that, whereas He was in the image of God, He emptied Himself and was made in the form of man, and then humbled Himself to die the death of the cross, being both human and divine.

They will believe and preach Christ as the only mediator between God and man, claiming that all blessings that have ever come from the hand of God to the human race have come through Him, and that through Him the whole creation was brought into existence. (John 1:1-3, 14; Col. 1:13-17; Heb. 1:1, 2.)

They will believe and preach Christ as the only true Advocate with the Father, offering His blood constantly in our behalf—our Intercessor, who presents for us the merits of His own sacrifice for sin.

They will believe and teach that the Bible is the only true, full, and complete revelation of God's will to men—His authoritative word.

They will believe and teach that the Holy Spirit is the only true vicegerent of the Son of God on earth; and will accept no other.

They will believe and teach the truth regarding the sanctuary—the true sanctuary, which the Lord pitched and not man; the heavenly sanctuary, in which the Lord Jesus is our High Priest; the sanctuary which was to be cleansed (Heb., justified, Dan. 8:14, margin) in 1844, the end of the long prophetic period of 2300 years.

They will believe and teach the truth concerning the true Sacrifice once offered on Calvary for the sins of the human race; and they will show that this one sacrifice for sin was sufficient, without the idolatrous sacrifice of the mass.

They will believe and teach the truth concerning the true priesthood of Christ, who was made a priest forever after the order of Melchizedek, a priest who stands at the head of the new creation, who, by offering Himself—interceding through His own blood in the heavenly sanctuary—is able to save unto the uttermost all who come unto God by Him.

They will believe and teach the truth concerning the necessity of confessing their sins to the High Priest above, and not to any earthly priest.

They will believe and teach the truth concerning the fullness of the forgiveness of the sins that are confessed to this High Priest, and the completeness of His cleansing of the sinner from all unrighteousness.

They will believe and teach the truth of true baptism; that it is a burial and a resurrection; that it typifies the complete death of the "old man" of sin,—"the body of sin,"—and its burial, and then a resurrection to "walk in newness of life."

They will believe and teach the truth concerning the true Communion, the Lord's Supper.

They will believe and teach the truth regarding the true law of God, which existed in the very beginning, was given in thunder tones on Mount Sinai, and is the perpetual standard of righteousness, the very foundation of the government of God.

They will believe and teach the truth regarding the true Sabbath, which was made by the Creator, and given, in Eden, to the human race as a perpetual memorial of the exercise of the creative power of God. They will discard the false and counterfeit Sabbath, as they will also all the counterfeits of the false system; and they will observe only the true Sabbath of Jehovah, the seventh day. This they will present as the sign between Jehovah and His people. (Ezek. 20:12, 20.)

They will teach also the truth of the nature of man, the state of the dead, the reward of the righteous, and the fate of the wicked, all of which have been perverted in the false system. Instead of preaching a purgatory, or a conscious state of existence in death, they will teach the truth of the Bible,—that the dead are unconscious (Ps. 146:3, 4); that "they know not anything" (Eccl. 9:5, 6); that man is mortal (1 Tim. 6:13-16; 1 Cor. 15:51-54); and that the time of rewards and punishments will take place, not at death or in death, but at the resurrection from the dead (2 Tim. 4: 8).

Thus this people, through whom God chooses to deliver His final message of truth, will believe and teach every truth that has been perverted in apostate Christianity. They will be guided in their work by the gift of prophecy. The message they will present to the world will obviously be opposed to the papacy, and therefore, when it is preached, it will constitute a great warning against "the beast and his image" and against the reception of his mark.

Inasmuch as this last church of Christ is the exact opposite of the system that Satan has designed shall take the place of the gospel, it is not to be wondered at that "the dragon" makes special war against this remnant, which "keep the commandments of God" and deliver the last message of God to the world. (Rev. 12:17.)

That this church which stirs the wrath of the dragon is the same as that which gives the warning message against the beast and his image is evident from the fact that it is described in almost identical terms. (Rev. 14:12; 12:17.) Those who give God's final message will be commandment keepers, and therefore will observe the seventh-day Sabbath.

This last message of the gospel, containing the full truth of God, will not be preached in a corner to just a few persons; it will be taken to all the earth, "preached in all the world for a witness unto all nations." When it has been taken to all the earth, Jesus will come the second time, and the great controversy between Christ and Satan will come to a final end.

Just such a people as are here described as the remnant church have been raised up, and they are now engaged in the very work called for in the prophecy— that of taking the final and complete message of truth to all the world. They are called Seventh-day Adventists.

A thoughtful study of this movement and its message, with the time of its arising, discloses the following facts:

It followed the churches of the Reformation, and has gone beyond them into advanced light.

It is in very truth delivering to the world the message of the coming of Christ.

It meets all the specifications of various prophecies regarding the last movement of the gospel.

It teaches the observance of the Ten Commandments, in fulfillment of these same prophecies.

It teaches Sabbath keeping.

It has had restored to it the gift of prophecy.

It is the very opposite of the papacy in fundamental principles.

It is preaching the warning message against the beast and his image.

All the fundamental truths of the gospel of Christ are contained in its message.

This movement is in very deed and truth what it purports to be—the final work of the gospel among men.

Satan has swept all the world into one deception or another. He has turned the truth of God into a lie, and has succeeded in getting men to believe that lie. His last attempt against the church of Christ will be made with the intention of destroying from among men this remnant, which is carrying the banner of truth to the world. He will bend all the energies of his master mind to the work of bringing these servants of God to destruction, and with them the truth they bear to the world.

He knows that he has but a short time in which to work. The controversy between himself and God, which began in heaven, is fast closing, and he realizes that what he does he must do quickly. He is determined to destroy the truth of God from the earth, and also the people of God. Therefore, "the dragon was wroth with the woman, and went to make war with the remnant of her seed, which keep the commandments of God, and have the testimony of Jesus Christ." Rev. 12:17.

But God himself is leading this people. He is their Head. He has given them counsel through the ancient gift of prophecy. Led by Him they will triumph, and finally stand on the sea of glass in His presence, singing the song of deliverance.

> "Here is the patience of the saints: here are they that keep the commandments of God, and the faith of Jesus." Rev. 14:12.

"And I saw as it were a sea of glass mingled with fire: and them that had gotten the victory over the beast, and over his image, and over his mark, and over the number of his name, stand on the sea of glass, having the harps of God." Rev. 15:2.

CHAPTER TWENTY

The Fulfillment of the Prophecy

IN the very year marked by the prophecy of the 2300 days, 1844, God restored the gift of prophecy to His remnant church in fulfillment of Rev. 12:17.

The time had come. The movement was about to begin that would carry to all the world in the last generation the truths of the threefold message, and raise up a people who would "keep the commandments of God, and the faith of Jesus." (Rev. 14:12.) Just before the disappointment of October 22, 1844, God gave a vision to a young man connected with the Advent movement of that time. His name was Hazen Foss. He lived in Poland, Maine. He was a strong believer in the message of the Lord's coming on October 22. He was a man of pleasing personality, good education, and of fine appearance, but of considerable timidity.

The Spirit of God came on this young believer, and gave him a vision of the future of the Adventist movement, and the trials of the coming experiences of the Adventist people. In connection with this view he was commissioned to deliver certain messages of warning. He was also permitted to see his own future experiences in case he faithfully carried out the mission upon which he was sent.

In his vision he saw a large platform, on which large numbers of people were standing, the Adventist people. Then these people stepped to a second platform, somewhat higher. Finally there was a third platform to which they moved, and this extended to the gates of the holy city itself. Those who advanced to this platform were joined by a great company of people, and finally from the level of this platform they entered the kingdom of God.

Mr. Foss did not understand this part of the vision. He expected the Lord Jesus to come in a very short time, on the completion of the preaching of the first and second angels' messages. This vision, understood later, disclosed the fact that a third message was to follow, and that it was on the platform of that message that the believers were to be taken into the kingdom.

Mr. Foss was commanded in the vision to make known to his fellow believers the information and instruction which he had received in this way.

Having been shown in vision the hardships he would be called upon to endure if he carried out God's mission for him, and being proud as well as timid, he shrank from the reproach that he knew he would have to suffer if he related what he had seen. Opportunity to relate his experience was presented to him in the meetings of the believers. He did not take the opportunity.

Then the vision was given him again, and on this occasion he was plainly told that should he still refuse to give the benefit of this divine instruction to the believers, this spiritual gift would be removed from him and conferred on another—one of the very weakest of the children of the Lord—who would carry out with fidelity and precision the mission given of the Lord.

Still Mr. Foss, though desiring to do God's will, permitted his pride and timidity to prevail. He did not tell his brethren the revelation he had received. Then the Lord spoke to him the third time, telling him he was released from the burden, which was laid now upon another, "one of the weakest of the weak," who would be faithful in doing the bidding of the Lord.

Frightened by the possibility that the Lord was forsaking him, the young man decided he would no longer allow his fears to deter him from carrying out the desire of his Lord. He called a meeting of his fellow believers. They responded and gathered together in meeting. He related his experience, telling them that the Lord had shown him a vision and commanded him to convey it to them, of how he had been rebellious, refusing to do as the Lord commanded. He told of the warning he had received of what the result of refusing would be, and that he still held back. He related the third experience, the word that he was now released, and how this nerved him on to relate the vision. "And now," he continued, "I will tell you what the Lord showed me, and what He wanted me to relate to you."

He opened his mouth to speak, but no words came. A surprised and startled look came into his eyes. In fear and anguish he finally cried out, "I cannot recall the vision. It is gone." Wringing his hands in his intense distress, he continued, "God has done as He said; He has taken the vision from me." He rushed out, crying, "I am a lost man."

Hazen Foss lived for nearly fifty years after this, but never again attended a meeting of the Adventist believers, or manifested any interest in religious things. It seemed clear that God had departed from him.

Shortly after this, it became apparent who it was that the Lord meant by the words "one of the weakest of the weak," and who it was upon whom He laid the burden of receiving the gift of prophecy. Among the believers there was a young woman, seventeen years of age, by the name of Ellen G. Harmon. She had accepted the Adventist teachings a few years previously, under the preaching of William Miller, though she had been an earnest Christian from early childhood. She was, at this time, in failing health, which had brought her to a serious condition. Her physician reported her to be afflicted with dropsical consumption, her right lung being decayed, and the left lung considerably diseased, while at the same time her heart was affected. So critical, indeed, was her condition that she had no hope of living very long. The physician said her life would be very short, and her condition was such that she might die at any moment. It was necessary for her to be propped in a semi-reclining position in order to breathe with any ease. Her physical strength was greatly reduced by constant spells of coughing and hemorrhages of the lungs. She was awaiting the day of her death.

It was to this suffering Christian girl that the Lord chose to reveal Himself and through her to restore the gift of prophecy to His remnant people. In December, 1844, Miss Harmon was staying at the home of one of the believers in Portland, Maine, a woman by the name of Haines. In the morning five women knelt in family worship in this home. Each one prayed, and lastly Miss Harmon began to pray, speaking only in a whisper, so weak was she. Suddenly, in the midst of her prayer, the power of God came down in a most striking manner, affecting every person in the room, as Paul's companions were affected on the road to Damascus when he saw his Lord (Acts 9:7), and as the attendants of Daniel were affected (Dan. 10:7). In a moment this slight, weak girl was carried away in her first vision, lost to all that was taking place about her.

In the next meeting of the Portland believers she told what she had seen in vision. Later she wrote it. These are her words: "While praying, the power of God came upon me as I had never felt it before. I was surrounded with light, and was rising higher and higher from the earth. I turned to look for the Advent people in the world, but could not find them, when a voice said to me, 'Look again, and look a little higher.' At this I raised my eyes, and saw a straight and narrow path, cast up high above the world. On this path the Advent people were traveling to the city, which was at the farther end of the path. They had a bright light set up behind them at the first end of the path, which an angel told me was the 'midnight cry.' This shone all along the path, and gave light for their feet, that they might not stumble. And if they kept their eyes fixed on Jesus, who was just before them, leading them to the city, they were safe. But soon some grew weary; they said the city was a great way off, and they expected to have entered it before. Then Jesus would encourage them by raising His glorious right arm, and from His arm came a bright light, which waved over the Advent people, and they shouted, Hallelujah! Others rashly denied the light behind them, and said that it was not God that had led them out so far. The light behind these went out, leaving their feet in perfect darkness, and they stumbled and got their eyes off the mark, and lost sight of Jesus, and fell off the path down into the dark and wicked world below. Soon we heard the voice of God like many waters, which gave us the day and hour of Jesus' coming. The living saints knew and understood the voice, while the wicked thought it was thunder and an earthquake. When God spake the time, He poured on us the Holy Spirit, and our faces began to light up and shine with the glory of God, as Moses' did when he came down from Mount Sinai."

About one week after her first vision Miss Harmon was given a second. She was then in her father's house. In this vision she was instructed, as Hazen Foss had been, to make known to her fellow believers what God had shown to her. Not knowing how she could carry out such a command in the weakened condition in which she then was, having, as she thought, but a short time to live, and suffering much actual physical pain, being unused to society and so naturally timid and retiring that it was painful for her to talk to strangers, she prayed most earnestly for days, often far into the night, importuning the Lord to remove this duty and lay it upon someone better fitted to perform it.

A third vision was given her, and she heard the words, "Make known to others what I have revealed to you." Determined to do the Lord's will, she consented. It was revealed to her that she should go to Poland, Maine, the home of Hazen Foss, and there narrate what she had seen. She did so, calling a meeting there in a private home. Hazen Foss was approached by one of the brethren and asked to attend this meeting. He would not consent to attend, being in despair, but he entered an adjoining room, and heard Miss Harmon relate what she had been shown. Hearing this, he said afterwards, "The vision she has related is as near like what was shown to me, and what I was unable to recall, as two persons could describe the same thing. That is the instrument on whom the Lord has laid this burden."

Miss Harmon did not die in the short time given to her by her physician. She lived, and continued to receive revelations from the Lord. During seventy years God used her in this important work, imparting instruction to her for the guidance of His great final message of the gospel. On August 30, 1846, she was married to Elder James White, one of the pioneer ministers of this movement, and ever since has been known affectionately by the people of the Adventist faith as "Sister White." She died July 16, 1915, eighty-seven years of age, after seventy years of earnest labor in many parts of the world as God's messenger. During this long period of time she was honored with many revelations from heaven. These she faithfully wrote out for the instruction of God's people. Her writings have filled many books, and these have been translated into many languages, and circulated by the hundreds of thousands in many countries of the world. She has been accepted as one possessing the genuine gift of prophecy by Seventh-day Adventists around the world. By these her experiences and work are believed to be in fulfillment of Rev. 12:17.

"We have heard from the bright, the holy land,
 We have heard and our hearts are glad;
For we were a lonely pilgrim band,
 And weary, and worn, and sad.
They tell us the saints have a dwelling there—
 No longer are homeless ones;
And we know that the goodly land is fair,
 Where life's pure river runs."

    —W. H. Hyde, written after hearing one
    of the early visions of the gift of prophecy.

CHAPTER TWENTY ONE

The Physical Tests Applied

THE believers in the Advent movement in the early days were not slow to apply to the manifestation of the gift of prophecy through Ellen G. Harmon the tests of the Bible. The fruits of this gift had not then developed, and the test, "By their fruits ye shall know them," had to be deferred until later. The physical tests pointed out in the Bible, however, were searched out, carefully and thoroughly applied, and successfully met.

An eyewitness, one who saw her in many visions, describes her condition in this way: "I have had the privilege of seeing her in vision about fifty times. I have been present when physicians have examined her while in this state, and I esteem it a pleasure to bear testimony to what I have seen and known. I trust a narration of the facts in the case may not be carelessly cast aside for the random suppositions of those who have never seen her in this condition.

"In passing into vision she gives three enrapturing shouts of 'Glory!' which echo and re-echo, the second, and especially the third, fainter, but more thrilling than the first, the voice resembling that of one quite a distance from you, and just going out of hearing. For about four or five seconds she seems to drop down like a person in a swoon, or one having lost his strength: she then seems to be instantly filled with superhuman strength, sometimes rising at once to her feet and walking about the room. There are frequent movements of the hands and arms, pointing to the right or left as her head turns. All these movements are made in a most graceful manner. In whatever position the hand or arm may be placed, it is impossible for any one to move it. Her eyes are always open, but she does not wink; her head is raised, and she is looking upward, not with a vacant stare, but with a pleasant expression, only differing from the normal in that she appears to be looking intently at some distant object. She does not breathe, yet her pulse beats regularly. Her countenance is pleasant, and the color of her face is florid as in her natural state."—*J.N. Loughborough, in "The Great Second Advent Movement," pp. 204, 205.*

The following statement of a physician regarding her condition in vision speaks for itself:

"Sister White [formerly Miss Harmon] was in a vision about twenty minutes or half an hour. As she went into vision every one present seemed to feel the power and presence of God, and some of us did indeed feel the Spirit of God resting upon us mightily. We were engaged in prayer and social meeting Sabbath morning at about nine o'clock. Brother White, my father, and Sister White had prayed, and I was praying at the time. There had been no excitement, no demonstrations. We did plead earnestly with God, however, that He would bless the meeting with His presence, and that He would bless the work in Michigan, As Sister White gave that triumphant shout of 'Glory! g-l-o-r-y! g-l-o-r-y!' which you have heard her give so often as she goes into vision, Brother

White arose and informed the audience that his wife was in vision. After stating the manner of her visions, and that she did not breathe while in vision, he invited any one who wished to do so to come forward and examine her. Dr. Drummond, a physician, who was also a First-day Adventist preacher, who (before he saw her in vision) had declared her visions to be of mesmeric origin, and that he could give her a vision, stepped forward, and after a thorough examination, turned very pale, and remarked, '*She doesn't breathe!*'

"I am quite certain that she did not breathe at that time while in vision, nor in any of several others which she has had when I was present. The coming out of the vision was as marked as her going into it. The first indication we had that the vision was ended, was in her again beginning to breathe. She drew her first breath deep, long, and full, in a manner showing that her lungs had been entirely empty of air. After drawing the first breath, several minutes passed before she drew the second, which filled the lungs precisely as did the first; then a pause of two minutes, and a third inhalation, after which the breathing became natural."—*Signed, "M.G. Kellogg, M.D., Battle Creek, Mich., Dec. 28, 1890."*

Every mark of a true prophet in vision, as given in the Bible, extreme weakness, open eyes, supernatural strength, and cessation of breathing, were all met in Miss Harmon's experience again and again, and to the satisfaction of her fellow believers. A signed statement by D. H. Lamson, Hillsdale, Mich., dated Feb. 8, 1893, thus describes his experience of a vision given her at Rochester, N.Y., on June 26, 1854:

"I was then seventeen years old. It seems to me I can almost hear those thrilling shouts of 'G-l-o-r-y!' which she uttered. Then she sank back to the floor, not falling, but sinking gently, and was supported in the arms of an attendant. Two physicians came in, an old man and a young man. Brother White was anxious that they should examine Sister White closely, which they did. A looking-glass was brought, and one of them held it over her mouth while she talked; but very soon they gave this up, and said, 'She doesn't breathe.' Then they closely examined her sides, as she spoke, to find some evidence of deep breathing, but they did not find it. As they closed this part of the examination, she arose to her feet, still in vision, holding a Bible high up, turning from passage to passage, quoting correctly, although the eyes were looking upward and away from the book,"

Another witness testifies thus:

"June 28, 1857, I saw Sister Ellen G. White in vision for the first time. I was an unbeliever in the visions: but one circumstance among others that I might mention convinced me that her visions were of God. To satisfy my mind as to whether she breathed or not, I first put my hand on her chest sufficiently long to know that there was no more heaving of the lungs than there would have been had she been a corpse. I then took my hand and placed it over her mouth, pinching her nostrils between my thumb and forefinger, so that it was impossible for her to exhale or inhale air, even if she had desired to do so. I held her thus with my hand about ten minutes, long enough for her to suffocate under ordinary circumstances; she was not in the least affected by the ordeal. Since witnessing this wonderful phenomenon, I have not once been inclined to doubt the divine origin of her visions."—*Signed, "D.T. Bourdeau, Battle Creek, Mich., Feb. 4, 1891."*

CHAPTER TWENTY TWO

The Test of Fulfilled Predictions

THE test of fulfilled predictions has been successfully met in the manifestation of the gift of prophecy given to Mrs. White. It is not, as has been pointed out, the chief factor in the exercise of this gift to foretell the future. There are occasions, however, when, in sending messages by revelation to His people, the Lord, for their encouragement, or as an incentive to activity and preparation, discloses coming events to them through this agency. All such predictions are exactly fulfilled when the time for their fulfillment arrives. Thus this test, laid down in the Bible in the words, "When a prophet speaketh in the name of the Lord, if the thing follow not, nor come to pass, that is the thing which the Lord hath not spoken, but the prophet hath spoken it presumptuously," has been fully met. (Deut. 18:22.) The falsity of a prediction, and of the gift that makes it, is demonstrated by the non-occurrence of the event foretold.

This is not the test of greatest importance, but it is by no means of slight importance. It has been applied many times to the work of Mrs, White, and never without being satisfactorily met.

In the year 1848 there began a movement that later

124 THE GIFT OF PROPHECY

was to attract world-wide attention. It is known today as Spiritualism. Then, at its beginning, it consisted of certain mysterious rappings and had not arrived at the dignity of having a name. It was confined to Rochester, N.Y., near which city it began. No one knew what it was, and no one dreamed of its later progress.

In the year 1850 Mrs. White wrote that she had received a revelation regarding this mysterious movement. This is what she said:

"Sabbath, March 24, 1849, . . . I *saw* that the mysterious knocking in New York . . . was the power of Satan, and *that such things would be more and more common, clothed in a religious garb* so as to lull the deceived to more security, and to draw the minds of God's people, if possible, to those things, and cause them to doubt the teachings and power of the Holy Ghost."—"*Early Writings,*" p. 35.

Seventeen months later she wrote this:

"August 24, 1850, I saw that the 'mysterious rapping' was the power of Satan; some of it was directly from him, and some indirectly, through his agents, but it all proceeded from Satan. It was his work that he accomplished in different ways; yet many in the churches and the world were so enveloped in gross darkness that they thought and held forth that it was the power of God. . . . *I saw that soon . . . it would spread more and more,* that Satan's power would increase, and *some of his devoted followers would have power to work miracles,* and even to bring down fire from heaven in the sight of men. I was shown that by the rapping and mesmerism, these modern magicians would yet account for all the miracles wrought by our Lord Jesus Christ, and that many would believe that all the mighty works of the Son of God when on the earth, were accomplished by this same power."—*"Early Writings,"* pp. 49,50.

When this prediction was made Spiritualism was scarcely known, and no one could imagine its later development. Today it numbers its adherents by many millions, and thus this prediction has been fulfilled.

Five years after this she wrote:

"I saw the rapping delusion—what progress it was making, and that if it were possible it would deceive the very elect. *Satan will have power to bring before us the appearance of forms purporting to be our relatives or friends now sleeping in Jesus. It will be made to appear as though these friends were present, the words that they uttered while here, with which we are familiar, will be spoken, and the same tone of voice that they had while living, will fall upon the ear.* All this is to deceive the saints, and ensnare them into the belief of this delusion."—*"Early Writings," Supplement,* p. 3.

This foretold the materialization of spirits, and spirit messages, at that time not practiced. Since then they have become the chief phenomena of Spiritualism. Forewarned by these gracious, enlightening messages from heaven, Seventh-day Adventists have not been deceived by spiritualistic trickery and deceit.

In 1890 a vision was given Mrs. White that led her to write the following predictions, which were published in the *Signs of the Times* of April 21, 1890:

"The tempest is coming, and we must get ready for its fury by having repentance towards God and faith toward our Lord Jesus Christ. The Lord will arise to shake terribly the earth. We shall see troubles on all sides. Thousands of ships will be hurled into the depths of the sea. Navies will go down, and human lives will be sacrificed by millions. Fires will break out unexpectedly, and no human effort will be able to quench them. The palaces of earth will be swept away in the fury of the flames. Disasters by rail will become more and more frequent; confusion, collision, and death will without a moment's warning occur on the great lines of travel. Oh, let us seek God while He may be found, call upon Him while He is near."

Here are things foretold that at that time seemed altogether incredible—increasing earthquakes, increasing trouble, thousands of ships hurled into the sea, navies going down, millions of human beings sacrificed, destroying fires increasing, and increasing railroad accidents. But we have seen their fulfillment since.

Who could have foreseen thousands of ships hurled into the sea when mines, torpedoes, and submarines were scarcely known, and their use on such a large scale as in the Great War unthought of? But literally "thousands of ships" were "hurled into the midst of the sea," during the Great War of 1914-18. And whole navies "went down." And "human lives" were in that conflict literally "sacrificed by millions." Nor are the other details of the prediction lacking in fulfillment all about us.

As far back as 1863 instruction was given by revelation to Mrs. White regarding the advantages of a simple, vegetarian diet and the use of natural, drugless remedies for the treatment of the sick, in which water treatments and the application of heat, cold, and light are used. She began then to write articles, which she continued until her death, regarding healthful living and the manner of practicing it, declaring that God had shown her the growth and development of a world-wide system of sanitariums based on these principles.

The medical world has scarcely caught up even now with the advanced light given this messenger of God. And, growing out of this instruction, just as foreseen, there is a chain of ninety-six sanitariums and treatment rooms belting the globe, practicing these life-giving and life-preserving principles which have come from heaven, and ministering to suffering men and women of many nations.

When the people of the Advent movement numbered about fifty in all, Mrs. White was shown in vision that, as the threefold message of Revelation 14, the commandments of God, and the faith of Jesus, were faithfully proclaimed to men, it would meet a welcome response on the part of many, and large numbers would embrace it and carry it to the ends of the world. Fulfilling that prediction today more than 300,000 Seventh-day Adventists have been raised up in the nations of the world, and are pressing their missionary and evangelistic activities in more countries than is any other mission organization, thus bearing the message of the Lord's return to all the earth.

In 1848 Mrs. White was given a revelation which she thus describes:

"At a meeting held in Dorchester, Massachusetts, November, 1848, I had been given a view of the proclamation of the sealing message, and of the duty of the brethren to publish the light that was shining upon our pathway.

"After coming out of vision, I said to my husband: 'I have a message for you. You must begin to print a little paper and send it out to the people. Let it be small at first; but as the people read, they will send you means with which to print, and it will be a success from the first. From this small beginning it was shown to me to be like streams of light that went clear around the world."'

In fulfillment of this prediction there are today fifty-nine publishing houses and branches in all the world, exclusively devoted to the publication of the threefold message, printing it in books, papers, pamphlets, magazines, and tracts in 141 languages. More than 400 languages are being used altogether in carrying this message in oral and written form. Evangelistic colporteurs numbering thousands are engaged in distributing this literature of the gospel of the kingdom, and it is, as foretold, "like streams of light" which go "clear around the world."

Beginning in the early seventies and based on instruction given in vision, Mrs. White began to urge the establishment of a separate system of schools, with an education based on the Bible, in which the young people and children of the Advent movement might be given a Christian education and prepare to become workers in bearing God's final message to the world. She declared that God had shown her that as these schools were started they would grow in number and be used of God to save the children and youth to the movement, safeguarding them against the errors and dangers of a false education, and providing an ample supply of laborers in the cause of God.

These predictions have been fulfilled in their entirety. Today, following the counsel thus given, there is an educational system connected with the Seventh-day Adventist movement, differing from everything in the world, comprising 204 advanced educational institutions, and 1,971 primary schools, scattered in every part of the world, giving Christian education to 89,833 young people and children, and providing the workers of this cause.

Yes, the test of fulfilled predictions has been fully and most satisfactorily met in the present-day manifestation of the gift of prophecy.

CHAPTER TWENTY THREE

The Gift of Prophecy Today

ALL of the tests prescribed by the Bible for the gift of prophecy have been applied to the work and experience of Mrs. E. G. White. As a consequence, this manifestation has been demonstrated to be the restoration of the genuine gift of prophecy in our day.

The supreme test, fidelity to the Bible, and loyalty to the Lord Jesus, has been met in all that Mrs. White has done, and said, and written, during a period of seventy years. She has exalted the Lord in it all, and the influence of her work and life have drawn all who have felt it nearer their Saviour. Her writings have deepened and enlarged the spiritual lives of her readers and illuminated their understandings in the blessed teachings of God's word.

In all that she has written and said, Christ is acknowledged, honored, worshiped, and upheld. She has been loyal to all that He taught, to all that He did, to all that He is, to all that He is to be. The whole influence of her life, her work, her writings, has been to exalt her Saviour, to glorify Him, to lead men to Him. She has been unfalteringly true to the historic Christ and historic Christianity, not swerving a hair's breadth from the great doctrines of the atonement, His pre-existence, His divine incarnation, His deity, His divine Sonship, His virgin birth, His miracle-working power, His divine authority, His substitutionary and expiatory death, His literal resurrection, His ascension, His mediatory and intercessory priesthood, His bodily, visible, personal, and imminent coming again.

She delighted to honor her Lord. In just one of her many books,—in all of which He is exalted and glorified,—she writes of Him as the Saviour of the world, our Advocate and Judge, the King who will reign in righteousness, the Anointed One, the Author of the resurrection, the Adored of the angels, the Seed of the woman, the Sent of God, the Author of truth, Shiloh the peace-giver, our Substitute and Surety, the Beloved of heaven, the coming Bridegroom, the Sin-bearer, the Sun of Righteousness, the Captain of the Lord's host, the Branch of David, the Good Shepherd, the I AM, the living Bread, the Lord our Righteous-ness, the Christ of God, the Exalted One, our Elder Brother, the First Fruits of the resurrection, the Foundation of the Jewish economy, the Daysman, the Deliverer, the Redeemer of the world, the Commander of the angels, the Conqueror of death, sin, and the grave, the Desire of all nations, the Consolation of Israel, the Creator of heaven and earth, the Divine Teacher, the Gift of God, the Door of the Sheepfold, the Friend of sinners, the Giver of manna, the Glory of Israel, the Great Physician, the Heart Searcher, the Heavenly King, the High Priest, the Image of God, the Holy One of Israel, the King of glory, the Judge of all the earth, the Hope of the fathers, the Lamb of God, the Majesty of heaven, the Light of life, the Messenger of the covenant, the Living Rock, the Lord of life and glory, the only-begotten Son, the everlasting Father, the Lord of the Sabbath, the Minister of the true tabernacle, the Prince of heaven, the Prince of life, the Prince of peace, the Prince of God, the Prince of sufferers, the Prince of light, the Promised One, the Resurrection and the Life, the Rock of faith, the Root and Offspring of David, the bright and morning Star, the Chiefest among ten thousand, the One altogether lovely, the Rose of Sharon, the Mighty God, the Shadow of a great Rock in a weary land, the Way, the Truth, the Life, the true Vine, the Wonderful Counselor, the world's rightful King, the true Sacrifice, the only and sufficient Saviour, and the Coming King.

All this He was to her. All this she sets Him forth to the world to be. All this He has become to many because of the gift God graciously manifested by her. *"Hereby know ye* the Spirit of God: Every spirit that confesseth that Jesus Christ is come in the flesh *is of God."* 1 John 4:2.

᾿ This is her counsel to every preacher, and she followed it herself:

"O that I could command language of sufficient force to make the impression that I wish to make upon my fellow laborers in the gospel. My brethren, you are handling the words of life; you are dealing with minds that are capable of the highest development. Christ crucified, Christ risen, Christ ascended into the heavens, Christ coming again, should so soften, gladden, and fill the mind of the minister that he will present these truths to the people in love and deep earnestness. The minister will then be lost sight of, and Jesus will be made manifest.

"Lift up Jesus, you that teach the people, lift Him

up in sermon, in song, in prayer. Let all your powers
be directed to pointing souls, confused, bewildered,
lost, to 'the Lamb of God.' Lift Him up, the risen
Saviour, and say to all who hear, Come to Him who
'hath loved us, and hath given Himself for us.' Let the
science of salvation be the burden of every sermon,
the theme of every song. Let it be poured forth in
every supplication. Bring nothing into your preaching
to supplement Christ, the wisdom and power of God.
Hold forth the word of life, presenting Jesus as the
hope of the penitent and the stronghold of every
believer. Reveal the way of peace to the troubled and
the despondent, and show forth the grace and
completeness of the Saviour."—"*Gospel Workers*,"
pp. 159, 160.

In its manifestation through Mrs. White, the gift of
prophecy has also been true to the Bible, and to all
that the former prophets have written. In all her
numerous books there is not one statement, one word,
that is contrary to the uniform teaching of the Holy
Scriptures. Its teachings she has consistently upheld
and inculcated. She looked upon Holy Writ as the
source of all truth, the guidebook of holiness, the
Word of the Living God. She wrote of it:

"The word of God is sufficient to enlighten the
most beclouded mind, and may be understood by
those who desire to understand it. But, notwithstanding all this, some who profess to make the Word of
God their study are found living in direct opposition
to its plainest teachings. Then, to leave men and
women without excuse, God gives them plain and
pointed testimonies, bringing them back to the Word
they have neglected to follow." "The testimonies are
not to belittle the word of God, but to exalt it and

attract minds to it, that the beautiful simplicity of
truth may impress all."

"Our watchword is to be, 'To the law and to the
testimony: if they speak not according to this word, it
is because there is no light in them.' We have a Bible
full of the most precious truth. It contains the alpha
and the omega of knowledge. The Scriptures, given by
inspiration of God, are 'profitable for doctrine, for
reproof, for correction, for instruction in
righteousness: that the man of God may be perfect,
thoroughly furnished unto all good works.' Take the
Bible as your study book."—"*Christian Experiences
and Teachings,*" p. 249.

To ministers, this was her instruction:

"Do not advocate theories or tests that Christ has
never mentioned, and that have no foundation in the
Bible. We have grand, solemn truths for the people. 'It
is written' is the test that must be brought home to
every soul. Let us go to the word of God for guidance.
Let us seek for a 'Thus saith the Lord.' We have had
enough of human methods. A mind trained only in
worldly science will fail to understand the things of
God; but the same mind, converted and sanctified,
will see the divine power in the Word."—Id., pp. 249,
250.

"To the law and to the testimony: if they speak not
according to *this word*, it is because there is no light
in them." Isa. 8:20.

The gift of prophecy, in its manifestation through
Mrs. E.G. White, has also been true to the law of God,
as were all God's true prophets. She wrote:

"When the law was proclaimed from Sinai, God
made known to men the holiness of His character, that
by contrast they might see the sinfulness of their own.

The law was given to convict them of sin, and reveal their need of a Saviour. It would do this as its principles were applied to the heart by the Holy Spirit. This work it is still to do. In the life of Christ the principles of the law are made plain; and as the Holy Spirit of God touches the heart; as the light of Christ reveals to men their need of His cleansing blood and His justifying righteousness, the law is still an agent in bringing us to Christ, that we may be justified by faith. 'The law of the Lord is perfect, converting the soul.'

"'Till heaven and earth pass,' said Jesus, 'one jot or one tittle shall in no wise pass from the law, till all be fulfilled.' The sun shining in the heavens, the solid earth upon which you dwell, are God's witnesses that His law is changeless and eternal. Though they may pass away, the divine precepts shall endure. 'It is easier for heaven and earth to pass, than one tittle of the law to fail.' The system of types that pointed to Jesus as the Lamb of God was to be abolished at His death; but the precepts of the decalogue are as immutable as the throne of God."—*"Desire of Ages,"* p. 308.

This gift has been true, too, to the Sabbath of the Lord, of which this has been written:

"'The Sabbath was made for man, and not man for the Sabbath,' Jesus said. The institutions that God has established are for the benefit of mankind. 'All things are for your sakes.' 'Whether Paul, or Apollos, or Cephas, or the world, or life, or death, or things present, or things to come; all are yours; and ye are Christ's; and Christ is God's.' The law of ten commandments, of which the Sabbath forms a part, God gave to His people as a blessing. 'The Lord commanded us,' said Moses, 'to do all these statutes, to fear the Lord our God, for our good always, that He might preserve us alive.' And through the psalmist the message was given to Israel, 'Serve the Lord with gladness; come before His presence with singing. Know ye that the Lord He is God; it is He that hath made us, and not we ourselves; we are His people, and the sheep of His pasture. Enter into His gates with thanksgiving, and into His courts with praise.' And of all who 'keep the Sabbath from polluting it,' the Lord declares, 'even them will I bring to My holy mountain, and make them joyful in My house of prayer.'

"'Wherefore the Son of man is Lord also of the Sabbath.' These words are full of instruction and comfort. Because the Sabbath was made for man, it is the Lord's day. It belongs to Christ. For 'all things were made by Him; and without Him was not anything made that was made.' Since He made all things, He made the Sabbath. By Him it was set apart as a memorial of the work of creation. It points to Him as both the Creator and the Sanctifier. It declares that He who created all things in heaven and in earth, and by whom all things hold together, is the head of the church, and that by His power we are reconciled to God. For, speaking of Israel, He said, 'I gave them My Sabbaths, to be a sign between Me and them, that they might know that I am the Lord that sanctify them,'—make them holy. Then the Sabbath is a sign of Christ's power to make us holy. And it is given to all whom Christ makes holy. As a sign of His sanctifying power, the Sabbath is given to all who through Christ become a part of the Israel of God.

"And the Lord says, 'If thou turn away thy foot

from the Sabbath, from doing thy pleasure on My holy
day, and call the Sabbath a delight, the holy of the
Lord, honorable; . . . then shalt thou delight thyself in
the Lord.' To all who receive the Sabbath as a sign of
Christ's creative and redeeming power, it will be a
delight. Seeing Christ in it, they delight themselves in
Him. The Sabbath points them to the works of
creation as an evidence of His mighty power in
redemption. While it calls to mind the lost peace of
Eden, it tells of peace restored through the Saviour.
And every object in nature repeats His invitation,
'Come unto Me, all ye that labor and are heavy laden,
and I will give you rest.'"—"*Desire of Ages,*" pp. 288,
289.

The test of fruitage, "by their fruits ye shall know
them," this manifestation of the gift of prophecy
meets with ease and success. "The Testimonies," or
writings of Mrs. E.G. White, together with her life,
her influence, her work, all reveal the Spirit of God,
and His constant guidance. They uphold and inculcate
the purest and loftiest morality. Every vice is discoun-
tenanced; every virtue is praised. They expose the devices and pitfalls of the enemy of our souls. They
safeguard against the perils in the pathway of the
Christian pilgrim. They warn against, and save from,
fanaticism. They turn the light of truth upon hidden
sins, disclose secret wrongs, bring evil motives to
light, lead to deep and lasting consecration, inspire to
holiness of life, influence to increased activity and
more intense zeal in doing the work of God.

These writings lead men to Christ. Their spirit is
that of the Bible. They exalt and glorify the Saviour of
men as the only hope of the world. They disclose to
us, in words that live and burn, the incomparable Life,

the immaculate Character, the unsurpassed Example of the Man of Galilee. With appeals that move and thrill and bring a response, they urge surrender to His exclusive control, and to consistent and holy living in following His example.

This gift in its present manifestation exalts the Bible. It emphasizes its divine origin and inspiration, and points men to it as the unalterable word of the Living God. It exhorts men to rest their faith and confidence upon it as the man of their counsel, the reliable rule of faith and practice. It entreats men to a close, a long, a diligent search of its sacred pages and truths in order to become familiar with its lofty teachings, which will judge them in the last day.

To thousands of weary souls this gift has brought relief, comfort, illumination, and hope. The weak have been strengthened, the feeble and fainting raised up, the lost guided to safety, the despondent cheered, the despairing made hopeful, the blind enlightened. Order has been brought out of chaos, crooked places made straight, dark things brought to light.

Truly, God has visited His people, so that they *"come behind in no gift*; waiting for the coming of our Lord Jesus Christ: who shall also confirm you unto the end, that ye may be blameless in the day of our Lord Jesus Christ." 1 Cor. 1:7, 8.